GANDHI AND THE NEW MILLENNIUM

GANDHI AND THE NEW MILLENNIUM

Ramjee Singh

Commonwealth

Gandhi and the New Millennium

Edition : 2021

ISBN 81-7169-635-X

Published by :
COMMONWEALTH PUBLISHERS (P) LTD.

Distributed by :
ARPAN PUBLICATIONS
4831/24, Prahlad Street,
Ansari Road, Darya Ganj,
New Delhi - 110002
Ph. : 23275511, 23257835
e-mail : commonwealthbooks@gmail.com

Typesetting by :
Rishu Computers
Delhi

Printed at :
Roshan Offset Printers
Delhi

Preface

Whether Gandhi is called the man of the new century or the man of the new millennium is irrelevant. Infact, he is a man beyond the millennium. 26 percent beliefs and policies continue, there is no meaning in welcoming either the new century or the new millennium. It might have special significance for Christians as the approximate bimillennium of Christianity. But the entry of the new millennium must be understood to be an anniversary of Earth to be enjoyed and celebrated by people of all faiths and all nations. It should be looked as a planetary "transitional" event, and as a "mega anniversary". Only then it can have potential for reinforcing the identify of human beings, first and foremost as citizens of Earth.

Gandhi, in fact, lived neither as *Hindu* nor as an *Indian* but like a citizen of the world. No doubt he obviously fought for India's independence but it was symbolic for the freedom of entire mankind. He had no ill-will against the Britishers from the beginning to the end. He was a devout Hindu no doubt, but he died for saving the life and dignity of non-Hindu who were in minority. So Gandhi has demonstrated through his personal life that narrow nationalism and sectarian religion cannot lead us to a safe future. If science is universal, religion must also be so or else religious fundamentalism will bring deluge on earth. So Gandhi provided a practical solution of treating all religion with equal respect (*sarva-dharma-sambhava*). A world-conquering religion through force or fear is no religion. Gandhi's religion had nither any geographical nor sectarian limits. For him, there is no religion higher than Truth and Righteousness. It was not the Hindu religion which he certainly prized above all other religions, but the *religion* which transcendo Hinduism, which changes one's very nature. Similarly, his nationalism, fierce though it is, is not exclusive, not designed to harm any nation or individual. His nationalism was never a peril to other nations nor it would exploit anyone. He wanted to see India free and strong so that she may offer herself as a willing and pure sacrifice for the betterment of the world. The better mind of the world desires today not absolutely independent states warring are against another but a federation of friendly interdependent states. In short, Gandhi's mission was "universal interdependence" and "Universal Religion". Hence he has been undisputedly claimed as the Man of the millennium.

I am extremely thankful to Mr. Ajay Verma of Commonwealth Publishers for choosing to publish this book as my humble gift of the millennium to my readers.

Ramjee Singh

Contents

Gandhi and His Fight for Peace

Chapter 1

PEACE IS NOT MERELY ABSENCE OF WAR

Peace is the happy, natural state of man; war his corruption, his disgrace. It is the evening star of the soul, as virtue is it sun; and the two are never apart. But peace is such as precious jewel that one should give anything for it but truth. Infact, "the way of peace is the way of truth. Truthfulness is even more important than peacefulness. A truthful man cannot long remain violent. So long as there is the slightest trace of violence in him, he will fail to find the truth he is searching.[1] Therefore, we can say that peace cannot stand without truth." False nations of propriety or fear of wounding susceptibilities often deter people from saying what they mean and ultimately land them on the shares of hyprocisy. But if non-violence of thought is to be evolved in individuals or societies or nations, truth has to be told, however harsh or unpopular it may appear to be for the moments".[2] Even the moral dictum *satyam bruyat, priyam bruyat na bruyat satyam apriyam* (speak truth, speak sweet; one had better not to speak it, if one cannot do so is a gentle way) means only that " There is no truth in a man who cannot control his tongue",[3] but this is no compromise with untruth. Hence where there is a choice between truth and non-violence, truth should prevail. But infact, basically there is no conflict between truth and non-violence. "Non-violence and cowardice go ill together".[4] True non-violence or truth is an impossibility without the possession of unadulterated fearlessness. To Gandhi, God is Truth and Love, God is fearlessness.[5]

However, truth is not merely a moral and ethical virtue, or a transcendental reality, it has also a societal character. Whatever is unjust is untruth. "Abstract truth has no value, unless it incarnates in human beings who represent it by proving their readiness to die for it".[6] For Gandhi, "truth and non-violence are no cloistered virtues but are applicable as much in the forum and legislatures as in the market place".[7] He did not agree with those who believed that *truth* has no place in politics and worldly affairs. Not only this, he tried to make truth not only matters for more individual practice but for practice by groups and communities and nations. It is no use of going about parothing truth and non-violence and steering clear of them in our daily life. To him, the attainment of national independence, eradication of untouchability, communal harmony and other constructive programmes were search after truth. Even his spinning wheel was an outward symbol of Truth. *Satyāgraha* is a relentless search for truth. The way of peace is the way of truth. These truthfulness is even more important these peacefulness. Intellectually, truth is openness of mind. In action, truth demands humility, tolerance but maximum fearlessness and sense of justice-individual and social. A social system or an economic structure which is based on injustice, inequality and exploitative. Truthfulness in speech is good but truthfulness in living and social behaviour is much more necessary.

Non-violence is also a wider concept than mere abstaining from overt personal injury. Peace does not dwell is outward things, but within the soul. If we have not peace within ourselves, it is in vain to seek it from outward sources. Emerson also said: "Nothing can bring you peace but yourself; nothing can bring you peace but the triumph of principles." Violence is a mental attitude manifesting a certain mode of behaviour, which, is most cases, is contacted from the environment. The ancient saints and seers, have been univocally emphasising non-violence as a great virtue. However, Gandhi, while accepting the personal basis of non-violence is word, deed and thought, has demonstrated its social and cultural aspects also. "The *rshis,* who discovered the law of non-violence in the midst of violence, were greater geniuses than Newton. They were greatest warrior than Wellington".[8] But Gandhi has also demonstrate that non-violence is a world-force. He has disproved the contention[9] "that these can be no non-violence rebellion". His accumulated experience of many decades convinced him that "non-violence is the most harmless and yet equally effective way of dealing with the political and economic wrongs of the down-trodden portion of humanity".[10] It is not a cloistered virtue to be practiced by the individual for his peace and final salvation, but it is a rule of conduct for society. Science of war leads one to dictatorship pure and simple. Science of non-violence alone can bad one to pure democracy.[11] Violent revolution has led to the rise of the dictatorship of Napolean in France, Cromwell in England, Stalin in Soviet Union, Zia-ul-Rehman Irshad etc. in B'desh. So he was constrained to believe that true democracy or the Swaraj of the masses can never come through the suppression or extermination of the antagonists. Individual freedom can have the fullest play only under a regime of unadulterated *ahimsa.*[12]

Non-violence, like truth, is as old as the hills. Gandhi's contribution has been to make non-violence a mass-weapon of fighting injustice and oppression. What was only an individual virtue, Gandhi has converted into a social weapon without the slightest neglect of its individual commitment.

Firstly, he views *Satyagraha* as a "moral equivalent of war". Gandhi's[13] "non-violence does not mean meek submission to the will of the evil-doer, but it means the putting of one's whole soul against the will of the tyrant".[14] He has opined: "Your, should not merely be a passive spirituality that spends itself is idle meditation, but if should be an active thing which will carry war into enemy's camp".[15] So he had rejected the word "passive resistance", because of its insufficiency and its being interpreted as a weapon of the weak.

Gandhi's concept of peace is both *religious* and *spiritual* as well as *socital* and *structural*. So far his religious and spiritual views are concerned, it *metaphysical, ethical* and *epistemological* strands. Metaphysically, if we can cultivate the attitude of "seeing all human being in the Self and the Self in all beings" (*Sarvatra Samdarsinah*)[16] or "seeing ourselves the same everywhere" (*Almaupamyena Samam Pasayati*[17]), we can achieve harmonious relationship with the universe.

Ethico-psychological basis of peace and non-violence is to transcend all strife and dispute, for "enemity is never anywhere appeared by enemity, but only by non-enemity.[18] Epistemological basis of non-violence may be the doctrine of non-absolutism (*Anekantavada*) and Relativism (*Syadvada*) "Courtesy towards opponents and eagerness to understand their view point in the ABC of non-violence".[19]

But more important than the metaphysical, the ethical and the epistemological basis of non-violence, Gandhi tried his best to bring out the structural dimensions of non-violence and war. According to him, the problem of war and peace is rooted in the very structure of our civilization, *i.e.*, in its technology, model of development, and structure of the State. He was convinced that violence is rooted in our societal structure. For example, industrialism has become a curse for mankind because it depends on our capacity to exploit on foreign markets, unhealthy competition and ultimately to wars. Besides, modern industrialism has been the greatest threat to human civilization because of ecological pollution, holes in the ozone layers and a fear of nuclear winter. Industrialisation inevitably leads of centralisation which is inconsistent with non-violent structure of society.[20] Infact, centralisation cannot be defended without adequate force.[21] On the other hand, "rural economy eschews exploitation altogether, and exploitation is the essence of violence.[22] E.F. Schumacher in his book "*Small is Beautiful*" has advocated the advantages of appropriate technology. Gandhi was not against machinery as such but against the craze of it.

Similarly Gandhi advocated 'production by masses' instead of 'mass-production'. What is necessary for India is not the "concentration of capital in a few hands, but its distribution so as to be within easy reach of 7.50 lakhs of villages".[23] In short, industrialisation can only cause concentration of money and labour and ultimately to exploitation and social violence.

"Economics of Peace" is *sine-qua-non* for a non-violence society. A centralised industrial society based on non-renewal source of minerals and energy breeds unhealthy competition and hatred among countries and violence against nature. This violence can at any moment turn into violence against one's fellowmen and as such there is today mad race for arms. Today, the military machine eats up more than 600 billion dollars per annum, when the half of world's population is suffering for want food, cloth and education. The development model adopted today is anti-peace and anti-people. Both capitalism and Marxism have implicitly accepted the common technological imperatives, resulting in centralisation, uninhabitable environment, unwieldy cities and violent society. We have to make a quantum leap is our intellectual perspective and develop an economy of disarmament and peace. Evils are inherent in industrialism and no amount of socialisation can eradicates them. Profit motive leads to large scale production, mechanisation and automation, cruel erosion of natural resources and profit motive.

As technology affect the model of development and economic structure, we need an appropriate non-violent political structure to control economic paradigm. No doubt, economics is the determining facts of our entire social system but everything including economy is under the State-power. Today, the State has grown and the individuals have suffered. Even the democratic socialist State remains a Leviathan.[24] The Welfare State has strengthened the grip of the State over the individuals. The idea of a transitional charactership is a myth. A people can choose a dictator they cannot order him to abdicate.[25] Modern science and technology have further strengthened the power of the State both militarily as well as from the point of view of the use of mass media. Hence, politics of non-violence needs a decentralisation political power. That Government is best which governs the least. The power of the state is embedded in the violent and coercive power. The State represent violence in the concentrated and organised form,[26] hence it can never the weared away from violence to which it owes its very existence. Politics based on structural violence has seeds of its own destruction through counter-violence. Hence unless we can develop the non-violent power of the people, and go on strengthening the physical force (*himsa-shakti*) or the force of law (*danda-shakti*), we cannot develop the politics of peace. What we need is people politics based on grass root partyless democracy rather than a party-politics rooted in manipulative seizure of power. Politics of Peace is also in conflict with militarism or narrow national chauvinism. We have to look upon the whole of humanity as one. These should be no limit to extending our services to our neighbours across State-made frontiers. God never made these frontiers. Nation States, are too narrow for the modern man who has conquered space. Hence, internationalism and a passion for world-peace is no utopia but on imperative.

However, politics is not everything. The scope of society is much bigger. Therefore, we have to encourage social equality, social justice, together with social harmony. Racial discrimination, aparthied, untouchability, casteism, communalism, and other forms of ethnic violence constitute the gamut of social violence. Unless these wrongful and violence-prone social structure is demolished. We cannot have a non-violent social order. Gandhi, through his 14 point Constructive Programme tried his best to fight out the roots of social violence. If the society is caste-ridden or race-ridden, caste or race riots are inevitable. Hence a casteless society is necessary. Gandhi fought most fiercely but non-violently the battle against communalism untouchability, sex-discrimination and religious orthodoxies. An unjust social order is bound to breed violence.

Lastly, we have both inherited a culture of violence and education based on the principle of structural violence. Due to educational omnipotence and misanthropic style is an important cause of violence. Defence of power, claims of authority, elitist privileges create structural violence in education. The quoted principles of education like obedience, drill, uniformity, order etc. are structural principles of violence. The violence of formal education is subtle but dangerous. Over and above, we have given prestige to the cult of violence by instituting syllabus in Military Science and Extension Programmes in Military Training like National Cadet Corpse etc. Education has income a vested interest and instrument of 'persecution of life', so it can never usher a peaceful society.

In the conclusion, we can definitely, say that both ideology and structure, are important for a non-violent social order. To say that if we can reform the individual and inculcate the spirit of love and non-violence, the society will become non-violent is only a half-truth. This effort to emphasise the importance of individuals has been continuing since the days of force. All religious saints and seers have been stressing the value of peace and non-violence but violence has become a way of life. It means that it is difficult to have a "moral man in a immoral society" or a "non-violent man in a violent society." Gandhiji had foreseen the role of both the individual and the social structure. It is simply an illusion to think of a 'paradise of peace' without a social structure of peace. No doubt, "the individual is the supreme consideration"[27] for Gandhi and he believed that "man is superior to the system"[28] but like a practical idealist, he wanted a non-violent socio-economic and political structure. Therefore, he was an ardent advocate of all-round social change and social justice.[29] When he wrote about the eleven Moral Vows,[30] his revolution was to improve the moral calibre of the individual look when he enunciated the 14 Points in his Constructive Programme, he had social transformation in mind. Non-violence demands a new desire, a new asceticism but it also needs an exploitation free, classless and free society. Life is a unity. These cannot die a water-light compartment between the individual and the social, economic and political, educational and social. In short, for non-violence, we need a total revolution-both in our mind as well as in our soul.

REFERENCES

1. Gandhi, M.K., *Gandhi Speaks,* ed. B.N. Mahton, Gaya, Institute to Socialist Education, 1973, p. 87.
2. Gandhi, M.K., *Harijan,* 19.12.1936.
3. Gandhi, M.K., *Young India,* 17.9.1925.
4. Gandhi, M.K., *Harigan,* 15.7.39.
5. Gandhi, M.K., *Young India,* 5.3.25.
6. Gandhi, M.K., *Young India,* 22.12.1921.
7. Gandhi, M.K., *Harijan,* 8.5.1937.
8. Gandhi, M.K., *Young India,* 11.8.1920.
9. Gandhi, M.K., *Young India,* 12.11.1931.
10. *Gandhiji's Correspondence with Government 1942-44,* Ahmedabad : Navajivan Publishing House, 2nd ed. 1945, p. 170.
11. Gandhi, M.K., *Harijan,* 15.10.38.
12. Gandhi, M.K., *Harijan,* 27.5.39.
13. Bose, N.K., *Selections from Gandhi,* Ahmedabad, Navajivan Publishing House, 2nd ed. 1957, p. 153.
14. Gandhi, M.K., *Young India,* 11.8.1920.
15. Gandhi, M.K., *Young India,* 12.5.1920.
16. *Isa Upanisad,* verse, 6,27.
17. *Sri Mad Bhagavadgita,* VI. 29-32.
18. *Dhammapada,* I.5.
19. Gandhi, M.K., *Hindustan Standard,* 20.7.1944.
20. Gandhi, M.K., *Harijan,* 18.1.1942.
21. *Ibid., Young India,* 12.11.1931.
22. *Ibid.,* 30.12.1939.

23. *Ibid.*, 23.3.21.

24. Narayan, J.P., *A Plea for the Reconstruction of Indian Polity*, Varanasi, A.B. Sarva Seva Sangh, 1959, p. 38.

25. Datta, A., *For Democracy*, p. 129.

26. Gandhi, M.K., *Harijan*, 10.12.1938.

27. Gandhi, M.K., *Young India*, 13.11.1924.

28. *Ibid.*, 4.8.1929.

29. Gandhi, M.K., *Mangal Prabhat.* (Hindi), Delhi, Sasta Sahitya Mandal, 1968.

30. Gandhi, M.K., *Constructive Programme*, (Hindi) Ahmedabad, Navajivan Prakashan, 1951 (Third riv. ed.)

Chapter 2

PEACE AND CONFLICT-RESOLUTION : INDIAN EXPERIENCE OF NON-VIOLENCE

The ideology of peace is rooted in the spiritual and cultural ethos of India. Not that wars and conflicts have not taken place here but they are its aberrations. Even the recent atomic tests, I am constrained to believe that they are against its legacy of peace and non-violence, notwithstanding its alleged strategic compulsions. The three great indigenous classical religions—the Vedic, Buddhism and Jainism univocally regard peace (Sānti) as the supreme virtue.

In fact, non-violence or peace grows out of its faith in spirituality. The same spirit is common to all in all mankind, nay even living beings. This is called "God in Man". Hence "the man with transcendental vision would be able to see all beings in the self only and the Self in all beings. Therefore he does not have any doubts, nor does he have any revulsions".[1] This idea of the Upanisad is further echoed in the Gita : "The man whose Self has been integrated by Yoga sees the Self in all beings and all beings in the Self; he sees the same everywhere".[2] The non-dualistic philosophy of Advaita Vedanta goes further to identify God with Man—That Thou Art[3] (*Tat Tvam asi*). Buddha also says : "Whosoever loves himself (and everyone does so) should not injure or harm others (who too likewise love themselves)". Realising that like oneself all beings seek happiness, one should not come in the way of other's happiness for the sake of one's happiness. So far Jainism is concerned, non-violence is its very core. According to the Jaina Scripture, non-violence is the foundation of all beings as the pure and eternal law.[4]

According to a great Jaina scholar Amritachandra Suri, all moral principles and practices are comprehended by Ahimsa (Non-violence). His argument is simple that since the principal desire of all beings is to continue to live and not to die, and all of them like happiness and avoid suffering, one who realises that all others are like oneself, ceases from violence, realising that other's pain and suffering are like those of oneself. The killing of another is indeed the killing of oneself, while compassion towards others is a compassion towards oneself. The special feature of Jainism is to extend the concept of non-violence to the field of knowledge and speech, known as the Theory of Non-absolutism (*Anekantavada*), and the Theory Relativism of Judgement and Speech (*Syadvada*). To think that my standpoint alone is true and correct and the rest are in the clutches of devils is the root cause of violence. The nature of reality is complex and human knowledge has limitations. Hence any claim of finality is illogical. We see things in fragment and from different angles of vision, so we can never think alike. Hence courtesy towards one's opponents and eagerness to understand their viewpoint is the ABC of non-violence.

Coming to the mediaval ages, the saints and surs like Guru Nanak, the founder of Sikhism, the Vaisnava saints of all varieties of the North and North-East India, Bengal, philosopher-saints of Maharashtra, the Alwars of the South have all univocally upheld the doctrine of peace and non-violence. In the modern times, we have Gandhi who has lived and died as a non-violent warrior.

Gandhi's ideology of peace and non-violence, though rooted in Indian spirituality and ethics has also been influenced by the non-violent martyrdom of Socrates for upholding truth, the life and death of extreme love and non-violence of Jesus Christ, total anti-strife and anti-war attitude of the Quakers, Tolstoy's interpretation of the *Sermon on the Mount,* Ruskin's *Unto This Last* and Thoreau's *Civil Disobedience.* He had a holistic view. He believed that "human society is not divided into watertight compartments called social, political and religious".[6] Human life being an undivided whole, no line can be ever drawn between its different compartments.[7] Besides, non-violence is not a cloistered virtue to the practised by the individual for his peace and salvation, but it is a rule of conduct for society. Thus Gandhi brought non-violence on the societal plane and also as moral equivalent of war[8] and violence.

In the Indian tradition, the concept of peace is multi-dimensional and holistic. The path of peace is the path of happiness and according to Buddha this is the state of immortality or salvation (*Nirvana*[9]). The final beautitude or Nirvana is described as the supreme blisful happiness.[10] Even Sankara identifies peace with liberation.[11] To approach peace is to become the Absolute.[12] It is complete cessation of all suffering. But it is not to be obtained by "desiring desires" but through reducing oneself of zero and through wisdom and abandonment of fruits of action.[13] This is what A.N. Whitehead says " the Harmony of Harmonies" which calms destructive turbulence and completes civilization. It is a positive feeling which crowns the life and motion of soul. It is broadening of feeling due to the emergence of some deep metaphysical insight, unverbalised and yet momentous in its coordination of values".[14] It involves "a grasp of infinitude", "the intuition of permanence" while its essence is "the attainment of truth", or "the conformation of purpose to the ideal beyond limitations". To Karl Jaspers, unless man's moral and political condition changes, he may physically perish. What is therefore required is the Rebirth of Man to prevent atomic doom.[15] Teilhard De Charden therefore emphasises the need to undertake concerted research leading to the pursuit of life to the very end provided the Christian and not the Faustian spirit is chosen.[16] Like the Indian thinking, even Freud is of the view that "unrest, unhappiness and anxiety" of contemporary men was due to their knowledge that with the help of their control over natural forces they could easily exterminate their whole race. This implies the necessity of self-control to overcome the craze to misuse control over nature. Russell also attributes the present predicament to our having learnt to understand and control the external forces to a terrifying extent but not those embodied in ourselves, which can be resolved only by self-control based on understanding of human needs.[17] To Einstein, our task must be to free ourselves from this prison (delusion) by widening our circle of compassion to embrace all living creatures and the whole of nature in its beauty.[18] This is like the Gita advising us to "abandon all desires and acts free from longing, without any sense of egotism for the attainment of peace".[19]

Today, when committed pacifists and peace-workers have been seriously engaged in peace-works, they are not serious about this fundamental dimension of mental or internal peace perhaps brushing it aside as outdated religious phenomena. This is true of the great work at Stockholm Institute for Peace Research, Sweden set up in 1966 and its SIPRI Year-book. Since wars begin in the minds of men, it is in the minds of that defence of peace must be constructed. But when there is no peace of mind, how can we think of peace? The West, in its glamour of achievements forgot to explore the secrets of the inner world because the contemporary western civilization is still rooted in Cartesian dualistic metaphysics. In its pride of science, they have come to despise and reject intuitive and instinctual perceptions that have come here to fore animated and given perspective and hope and meaning to human existence. We need a new instrument of thought and a perception of the "unbroken wholeness".

The Indian approach is to emphasise both the subjective and the objective conditions of peace. Peace is not just the absence of war. The ideology of Pax Mundi necessarily implies a Pax Mundi in the field of our life-style and societal structure. In short structural peace is as important as the peace of mind. Minds of men do not work in vacuum. They are conditioned by structure of society. Hence, unless our socio-economic and political systems together with educational and cultural systems are not re-oriented towards peace, our minds cannot grasp it properly. Even our societal structure is determined by our technological structure as technology and ideology often go together. Hence technological dimension has to be taken into consideration.

Considering this total framework, Arnold Toynbee predicted that the human spirit would rebel against the global unification. It will be a spiritual rebellion and this rebellion will start in India.[20] Going further he said : "a chapter which had a western beginning will have to have an Indian ending if it is not to end in the self-destruction of the human race".[21]

I cannot say that how far India is worthy of this compliment because today India has become more materialist than the west. So India wants to be a military power for fear of foreign invasion or incursion. But Gandhi had said : "the sword is entirely useless for holding India".[22] Hence the real Indian way is the way of non-violence. Hence Toynbee reiterates "At this supremely dangerous moment in human history, the only way for mankind is the Indian way—Emperor Ashoka's and Mahatma Gandhi's principle of non-violence and Sri Ram Krishna's testimony to the harmony of religions".[23]

Let us understand, what is the *Indian Way*? From the time immemorial, India has opted for a man-centred agro-rural industrial technology and a decentralised economy in contrast to large-scale to large-scale industrialisation and mass-production, centralised urban factory structure and market-oriented economy. In U.S.A. and other so-called advanced countries, agriculture is no longer a dominant sector. It has shrunk to less that 10% of its economy. The U.S.A. with a world population of about 6% consumes about 40% goods whereas about two-thirds of humanity is ruling and poverty, malnutrition, illiteracy etc. Hence, this globalisation is only so-called, it is diluted capitalism and illfarism. The Indian Nobel laureate Dr. Amartya Sen is right when he says that globalism with welfare is meaningless. His conception of development economics is based upon the welfare of the poorest people in society. Whether it be industrialised countries like U.S.A. or U.K. or developing countries like India and Kenya, a serious problem is unemployment. Unless we voluntarily curb our needs, we shall continue mercilessly exploiting nature and inviting environmental hazards like death holes in the ozone layers. Hence, we are constrained to go "not for *mass production* but *production by the masses*". Even Alvin Toffler, the author of *Future Shock* and *The Third Waive* has come out with the exciting concept of the "Electronic Cottage" and E.I. Schumacher speaks of *Small is Beautiful*. Toffler visualises that production will shift again from the factory back to the home. This is what is the Indian Way in Economics.

So far political dimension is concerned, Indian mind treats politics as an ethical cum religious enterprise where the State-craft is not an apparatus of power but of selfless social service. Hence, there is the conception of an ethical state and civil polity. The ideal of state is where there is the least crime or punishment and hence "the least government", there is self-rule or Home Rule instead of policy or military rule. The structure of polity is bound to be towards maximum decentralisation of power, participatory democracy at the grass-root, consensus polity, and aspiration towards world-fraternity. Religious fundamentalism, national chauvinism and militarism are not rooted in the Indian psyche. Even now when there are theocracies flourishing in and around our neighbourhood, India has stuck to the path of secularism. When nation-states are posing serious danger, India still thinks that we are living in One World. We have a common destiny. The whole world is a family. Even at present, we listen to salex-rattling between India and Pakistan. The voice of sanity and peace proposing a fraternity, federation or confederation between the two nations are being heard. Not to speak of Gandhi, even in post-Gandhian era, Jaya Prakash Narain, Dr. R.M. Lohia and last but not the least Acharya Vinoba Bhave, the spiritual heir of Gandhi have strongly advocated some sort of common political structure between India and Pakistan. The South Asian Group, the Asian People Association etc. are making useful efforts to establish people to people goodwill between the two countries. Similarly, then "Indian Way" is against militarism and war as they are enemical with peace and non-violence. We banish violence or war, not because of the threat of a Nuclear Winter or in view of threat: "Either we abolish war, or war will abolish us" but because peace and non-violence is ingrained in the cultural poyche of India. Today, the world has started realising that non-violence is the only way out. Martin Luther King says : "The choice before mankind is between non-violence and non-existence". Indian mind opts for non-violence as its faith or creed, not as compulsion. If Ashoka following Lord Buddha's teachings had established a non-violent state. India under Gandhi's leadership fought a war of independence and social discrimination through non-violence and Vinoba Bhave had ushered an aggrarian reform movement through non-violence and compassion. Even most recently Jaya Prakash Narain had galvanised the Indian polity and fought against suppression of civil rights during 1974-76 through non-violence.

Like structural non-violence in the field of Economics and Politics, Indian mind has been always conscious of incorporating the element of peace and non-violence in the field of education. Of course, there is no systematic syllabii on peace-education as we find today in the West, but there are very many social teacher in the form of saints and seers, whose non-formal teachings of peace are of greater value than syllabii in the educational courses. For example, besides Buddha's teachings of compassion, Mahavira's message of non-violence and Vedic-Upanisadic emphasis upon the ethics of peace, we have in recent times the demonstration of many objective lessons in the power of non-violence. We have witnessed the herald of Bhoodan (land-gift) movement, the non-violent movement against felling of tress in the Himalayas, movement against big dams and exploitation by multi-national companies.

In India, the outlook of life and the style of living together with the societal structure are so designed that it does foster non-violence. Non-violence is the law of Indian life as violence is the law of the jungle. In practical life, non-violent resistance is nothing but the law of self-sacrifice. "The *rishis,* who discovered the law of non-violence in the midst of violence, were greater geniuses that Newton and great warriors than Wellington. Having themselves known the use of arms, they realised their uselessness and taught a weary world that its salvation lay not through violence but through non-violence".[23] In recent times, Gandhi's ambition was to provide an instance, and it was his dream that his country may win its freedom through non-violence".[24] He did so not without knowledge but with "sixty years experience" behind him.[25] His accumulated experience of so many years filled him with the greatest hope that "in the adoption of non-violence lies the future of India and the world". Non-violence is the most harmless and yet equally the most effective way of dealing with the political and economic wrongs of the downtrodden portion of humanity is to live consistently with human dignity and make progress towards the attainment of peace".[26] Of course, the history of non-violence as an instrument of peace can be traced in India to pre-Buddhist times but search for peace continues and Mahatma Gandhi may be said to be the latest among the greatmen of wisdom who not only preached truth and non-violence but also lived them. Following Gandhi's examples, India has witnessed some magnificent demonstration of non-violence even after his martyrdom. Taking both Gandhian and Post-Gandhian experiences of peace and conflict-resolution. We can classify them as follows :

(a) Non-violent war of India's Independence.

(b) Non-violent Resistance Movement against Economic Injustice.

(c) Non-violent Resistance Movement against Social Injustices.

(d) Non-violent Resistance Movement in the form of Constructive Programmes.

(e) Peace-work and Peace-Army (Santi Sena).

It will be surprising to the western peace-workers and peace-scientists that except some isolated efforts by some groups in India, there is perhaps no obvious organised efforts toward Pax Mundi or world-peace. There are two reasons : Firstly, India had not the awful experience of ravages of World War I or II like the western nations. Secondly, the concept of peace is an accomplished and accepted notion of its culture so that it hardly needs to be discussed or debated. Thirdly, to the Indian mind, peace is a state of positive and constructive world-view and world-order, where individuals, groups and nations eschew to dominate or exploit each other and live in cooperation and mutual-aid. This means that peace needs a new life-style and a new culture. However, such a philosophy of civilization of peace does not work in a vaccum.

On the common theistic religious plane, the individual self is regarded as the part of the same spiritual entity called God. Hence, any conflict is regarded as anti-spiritual. The whole world is regarded as one's family. Similarly, the Indian mind has by and large adopted a technology with human face. So, they have an Economics of Peace, and Politics of Peace and so on.

Of course, the most characteristic development in the ideology of non-violence has been the use of non-violence in India's war of independence. It is almost assumed that in case of war of independence there should be no qualms about violence or non-violence. Freedom battles of all times and all countries have been eulogised as the epics of human valour. But India under Gandhi's leadership has shown novel way of struggle.

(a) India's long battle of freedom is a saga of courage and valour through non-violence. I propose to cite only four majestic examples, which had brought tremendous upheaval on national scale. After the Ist World War, when the British imperialist power refused to grant even 'Dominion Status' to India as per its own commitment and instead enacted a mass-genocide at Jalianwala Bagh and then imposed unjust Black Laws known as Rowlett Act to suppress freedom of expression and protests, Gandhi had launched in all India Non-cooperation Movement with tripple-boycott-strategy : foreign goods, foriegn courts and foreign educational institutions during 1921-22 in which hundreds were killed and thousands of people were imprisoned. I can compare it with Korean War of independence against the Japanese in 1919 under the leadership of popular Korean monk Rev. Han Yong-Un. The characteristic feature of the Non-cooperation Movement is that though there is no disobedience or defiance of the established laws, it is the most effective invisible war to shake the very foundation of British imperialist occupation through economic, political and cultural boycott. After a decade, in 1929-30, Gandhi's non-violent struggle assumed a more challenging dimension by giving a call of Civil Disobedience through wilful defiance of unjust laws. In 1940, in order to gauge the preparedness of the people for a full-fledged struggle, Gandhi started a peculiar non-violent method of Individual Civil Disobedience. In 1942, the struggle for Independence known as Quit India movement was launched. This led to Independence of India in 1947. By and large, all these movements were non-violent mass movement.

(b) Besides these above mass Civil Disobedience movements for India's independence, Gandhi had also organised non-violent resistance movements against economic injustices on local basis in different parts of the

country with exemplary success like in Champaran (1917), Kotagarh (1921), Borsad (1923) Vykom (1925), Kheda (1926-27), Bardoli (1928), Salt Satyagraha and Dandi March (1930). The story of every movement is the story of non-violent heroism of the Indian massess. In 1917, Gandhi had also taken up the cause of the textile labourers of Ahmedabad which resulted in a massive strike and then an honourable compromise.

(c) Apart from his fight against aggrarian and factory labourer's exploitation, Gandhi had his eye on social injustices and discrimination. Taking the clue of his non-violent struggle in South Africa against racial discrimination, he also started a non-violent movement to root out the evil of untouchability, discrimination and oppression against women. For him, Swaraj (independence) was synonymous with the establishment of the kingdom of Righteousness on earth.[27] He started campaign for temple entry to the untouchables and did a lot for their upliftment.[28] Similarly, he stood against various kinds of discrimination and oppression against women in society like the removal of veil,[29] child marriage,[30] compulsory widowhood,[31] dowry system,[32] prostitution, Devadasi system (compulsory concubine system attached to the temple priests), illiteracy etc.

(d) Constructive Programme—Apart from non-violent direct action of various kinds under the broad nomenclature of Satyagraha, Gandhi had introduced various Constructive Programmes for social change. Civil Disobedience, is an aid to Constructive Programme and *vice versa*. On the other hand, Constructive Programmes are imperceptible but most effective method of social change without any direct confrontation. Hence they may be described as the Gandhian way of conflict-resolution. Out of the 18 constructive programmes envisaged and launched by Gandhiji, they can be

classified under four heads : (1) Social, (2) Economic, (3) Educational and (4) Cultural. For Example, programme of communal harmony, Removal of Untouchability, Upliftment of Women and Adivasis are very potent programmes of social harmony and nation-building. Similarly, his stress upon Khadi and other Village Industries, Economic equality, Kisans, Labour are important dimensions for development and rooting out economic injustices. So also his programmes of Basic Education, Adult Education, Provincial Languages, National Languages and Students are important programmes to remove educational backwardness. Lastly, his insistence on Prohibition, Education in Health and Hygiene, and Village Sanitation are related to Cultural rejuvenation.

(e) Peace-work and Peace Army (Santi Sena) : Peace Army is the most important programme of peace-work and conflict-resolution, as envisaged and acted upon by Gandhi, Vinoba and Jaya Prakash Narain. In his Last Testament, Gandhi had visualised a confrontation between the Civil Power and the military power of police. He was convinced that if we allow to strengthen the police and military power, democracy will be dead. Hence in order to strengthen the civil-power he floated an organisation called Santi Sena or Peace Army. Even to Martin Luther King (Jr.) this (Santi Sena) "alone will back from the percipice".[33] Professor Glenn D. Paige of the Centre of Non-violence at Hawie, who had a close look at Santi Sena found great potentials in it. He said : "The future of mankind is not certainly in the hands of the soldiers of the army, but in the hands of the Santi Sainiks".[34] Now many countries have realized the need of exploring the possibilities of forming Peace Brigades to solve their problems of conflicts. Gandhi was both the commander and soldier of peace. As a Commander, he issued the order to "do or die" for maintaining peace and

as a Soldier he obeyed it and bacame a martyr. In a multi-racial, multi-religious and multi-lingual country like India, a civilian force like the Santi Sena is an imperative.

Other Examples of Peaceful Struggle and Conflict Resolution

After independence, when Gandhi was no more and when there was a bloodbath in Telegana region of Andhra Pradesh between the landlords and the landless people helped by the communist activists, it was again Acharya Vinoba Bhave, Gandhi's spiritual heir, who started land-gift movement and collected more than six million acres of land to be distributed among the downtrodden humanity. This movement also flourished into a holistic development movement of villages called Gramdan. He tried to develop consensus politics, rural development, communal harmony etc. Jaya Prakash Narain also joined this movement and added many valuable dimension like establishing Peace accord in Nagaland and Kashmir. Both Vinoba and Jaya Prakash Narain worked for conflict resolution and peace in many difficult areas of communal riots in Bihar, Bhillai, Rourkela etc. through Santi Sena. Vinoba and J.P. both had tried a lot to have friendship and peace with Pakistan and China. During great language controversy and widespread arson and violence including a dozen cases of self-immolation, it was again the sobering influence of Vinoba Bhave and J.P., which brought peace in India. Even today, Sri Narayan Desai, the son of Gandhi's most beloved Private Secretary Late Sri Mahadeva Desai is very serious about spreading Santi Sena. The entire Sarvodaya movement is against communalisation and criminalisation of Indian politics, as well militarisation including atomic blasts. Conflict-resolution and peace is not a matter of policy but of creed and faith for millions of people and dozens of organisations in India.

Even during last three decades, India has seen isolated but powerful non-violent movements like the *Chipko* against felling of trees in the Himalayan region under the able leadership of Sunderlal Bahuguna, Chandi Pd. Bhatt and others. There has been another powerful non-violent upsurge against construction of big dams thus displacing thousands of poor inhabitants and damaging the ecological balance under the leadership of Baba Amte and the dynamic desciple Ms. Medha Patkar. In Rajasthan, a young man Sri Rajendra Singh has fought a grim non-violent battle against carving stones from Aravalli mountains. On the aggrarian front, in Madras under the stewardship of Sri S. Jagannathan, we have seen a splendid non-violent resistance movement against the multi-national companies to grow see fishes on the fertile agriculture land and thus turning the entire sea-coast into desert only after a decade. Earlier, this very Jagannathan had staged a Satyagraha for distributing thousands of acres of land owned by the temple lords among the landless people. At present, the National Alliance, a combination of many non-political constructive groups, has been spearheading its movement against spreading the tantacles of multi-national companies, mostly of whom are here fore exploitation through increasing the cult of consumerism and destroying the age-old man-centred fabric of agro-rural industries and thus increasing unemployment. This is like the rebirth of Swadeshi movement, which aims at use of home-made things manufactured by our neighbours. "Swadeshism is not a cult of hatred but a doctrine of selfless service, that has roots in the purest love (Ahimsa)".[35] If Bible teaches "Love thy neighbour", Swadeshi also teaches the same. Besides, we have seen massive non-violent political movements on large scale in Assam in the Seventies.

Conclusion

Violence has lost its dynamics, no doubt but non-violence has not taken its root because violence is rooted in our societal structure and also in our mental make up. True India has a great legacy of peace and there has been an unbroken tradition of non-violent resistance against injustice but modern India is fast developing its option for consumerism and materialism. Hence, it is failing in its rightful obligation to take the initiative in global peace. Even the civic life of India has become highly violent. During the partition of the country, it has witnessed the worst violence and that has erupted off and on during communal and caste riots, linguistic tensions and so on. We have worst and the most vulgar show of hatred and public violence in case of demolition of the disputed structure of a Mosque. The entire North-East region is under turmoil and criminal violence and state violence go unabated. Even in Central India in Andhra and Bihar, violence has been reigning supreme. There has been so much of criminalisation of politics and politicalisation of criminals that even the normal democratic fabric seems to be in danger.

But again I dare say that these things have not touched the heart and soul of India. Even now more than 99% people want to live in peace and harmony. Overt violence is more due to structural causes like grim and growing poverty (60% people are living below the line of poverty), unemployment (about 300 million people suffer on account of unemployment and under-employment), caste and communal politics and so on. Thanks to our tradition of peaceful co-existence, that even after half a century, there has been no disintegration like Pakistan/ Bangladesh, Yugoslavia, Soviet Union; democracy however imperfect, is safe. Even secularism is living with vitality, when we find religious theocratic States all round us. Hence eruption of occassional violence is due to some structural and political causes. It is not in India's nature to practice violence. It is aberration.

Hence for peace in India, we have to gear up to banish poverty and unemployment as soon as possible. For this, for a country with a huge population of 1000 millions and small capital, a high-technology economy is unsuitable. We have to adopt agro-rural industrial decentralised economy to generate more employment. Since, politics is overall controller of our social system, it has to be given an ethical and moral base. Only a value-based politics or goodness politics can help to create an atmosphere of peace.

But we must realise that in this total crisis of the nation, education has its more than half its share[36] (as only 50% people are literate). However, neither our educational policy nor the Indian scholars have paid enough attention to some of the efforts and initiative for peace which should have been forthcoming from them by virtue of rich tradition of peace India has given to the world".[37] No field is more fertile and effective than education to develop the science of non-violence. But more academic approach is not enough. For this, training in Peace-Science and Peace-action is essential. It would be shocking to learn that out of 232 Universities in India, only 8 or 9 provide teaching and research in Gandhian Thought and Peace. Similarly, whereas almost all universities and High Schools have introduced military training (N.C.C. or A.C.C.) as extension programme, they have not thought it feasible or worthwhile to induct Santi Sena or Peace Brigade training. This shows not only callous disregard for peace but also intellectual bankrupcy. India is spending millions of rupees on police and para-military forces for maintaining internal peace but crime graph is rising. The only way out to maintain peace is to introduce Santi Sena Scheme in every village or Mohalla of the city. It is height of our cynicism that we still do not believe that the law of love is the single tool for solving conflict. We wrongly think that we have a tendency to make war which we have inherited from our animal ancestor and we are genetically oriented towards committing violence. But Serville "Statement on Violence" (6.5.1986) has declared it as scientifically incorrect. Hence there is no scope for biological or psychological pessimism. But though violence has failed thousand times, we have not as yet been disillusioned. But India has the experience of the power of non-violence from time immemorial. It is the crest jewel of its culture. It has sustained India so long and it will continue to sustain in future because India without non-violence is not India.

REFERENCES

1. *Isa Upanisad,* verses 6 & 7.
2. *Bhagavadgita,* VI.29, 32.
3. *Vedanta Sutra* (Sankara Bhasya), IV.1.3. We can compare it with Quaker's doctrine according to which there is in everyman's inmost being the Inner Light.
4. *Acharanga Sutra,* 1.3.3; 1.3.5.
5. Murty, S., *The Quest of Peace,* Delhi, Ajanta Publications, 1986, p. XIX.
6. Gandhi, M.K., *Young India,* 2.3.1922.
7. *Ibid., Harijan,* 30.3.1947.
8. *Ibid., Yound India,* 5.11.1931.
9. *Dhammapada,* 285.
10. *Bhagavadgita,* VI.15.
11. Sankara, *Gita Bhasya,* II.70.

12. *Ibid.*, VI.15; II.27.
13. *Bhagavadgita*, II.70-71.
14. Whitehead, A.N., *Adventure of Ideas*, Pelican Books, 1948, p. 327.
15. Jaspers, Karl., *The Future of Mankind*, Chicago, 1961.
16. Teilhard De Charden, *The Future of Man*, London, 1964.
17. Russell, Bertrand, See *Authority and the Individual*, London, 1949, pp. 112, 125; *The Impact of Science on Society*, London, 1952, pp. 113-114.
18. Einstein, Albert, Letter to Max Bora.
19. *Bhagavadgita*, II.71.
20. Toynbee, A., Address to the Philosophy Club at Cambridge University, 1952 on the topic "2002" quoted by A. Aram, Towards 2000 A.D., Madurai, Peace House Publications, 1986, p. 28.
21. *Ibid.*
22. Gandhi, M.K., *Hind Swaraj*, Ahmedabad : Navajiwan Press, Rev. 2nd ed., Seventh Reprint, 1989, p. 36.
23. *Ibid.*, p. 29.
24. Gandhi, M.K., 11.8.20.
25. *Ibid.*, 12. 11.31.
26. *Ibid.*, *Harijan*, 24.2.1926.
27. Gandhi's correspondence with the Government 1942-44, Ahmedabad : Navajiwan Publishing House, 2nd ed., Sept. 1945, p. 170.
28. Gandhi, M.K., *Young India*, 4.5.21.
29. *Ibid.*, *Young India*, 27.4.21; 4.5.21; *Harijan*, 20.4.34; 23.3.47.

30. *Ibid.*, 3.2.27; 25.11.26, *Harijan*, 23.3.47.

31. *Ibid.*, *Young India*, 11.26; 15.9.27.

32. *Ibid.*, *Young India*, 5.8.26; 15.9.27.

33. *Ibid.*, *Young India*, 27.12.28; *Harijan*, 23.5.36; 16.3.47.

34. Radhakrishnan, N., "Higher Education and Training in Non-Violence : The Santi Sena of G.R.I.", *Facets of Educational Policy*, Gandhigram, 1966, p. 41.

35. *Ibid.*, p. 42.

36. Gandhi, M.K., *With Gandhiji in Ceylon*, by Mahadev Desai, Madras, S. Ganeshan, 1928, p. 108.

37. Rammurti, Acharya, *A Perspective Paper on Education*, New Delhi, 1990, p. 11.

38. Agrawal, M.K., "*Peace Education in the Context of Global Crises*", Gandhi Marg, New Delhi, G.P.F., July-Aug., 1984.

Chapter 3

STRATEGIES FOR PEACE-MAKING AND CONFLICT-PREVENTION

1. Prayer, Preaching and Precept

Faith cannot be developed except through prayer. Non-violence succeeds only when we have a living faith in God"—says Gandhi.[1] Human effort must be there always... All this and much more along the same line can never be a substitute for prayer. But one may ask, "Why pray at all? Does not God, if there be one, know what has happened? Does he stand in need of prayer to enable Him to do His duty?" The answer is —"No, God needs no reminder. He is within everyone. Nothing happens without His permission. Our prayer is a heart search. It is a reminder to ourselves that we are helpless without His support... Prayer is a call to humility. It is a call to purification, to onward search".[2] In its simplest definition, prayer is merely a wish turned God-ward. The deepest wishes of the heart find expression in secret prayer. "Prayer", says St. Jerome, "is a groan". The very cry of distress is an involuntary appeal to that invisible Power whose aid the Soul invokes.

Prayer is not eloquence, but earnestness. In prayer it is better to have a heart without words, than words without a heart. A popular preacher once said of his pulpit efforts, "I always roar when I have nothing to say." To love to preach one thing — to love those to whom we preach, quite another. Pulpit discourses have insensibly dwindled. It is a good divine that follows his own instructions. The defects of a preacher are soon spied. "It is better to allow our lives to speak for us than our words." God did not bear the Cross only 1900 years ago, but he bears it today".[3] Crucification of Christ is more powerful than the innumerable sermons delivered from the pulpit so far. An ounce of action is better than tons of words. What is faith worth if it is not translated? Hence Gandhi advises: "Do not then preach the God of history, but show Him as He lives today through you".[4] He further said: "My life is my message." It means that even a lofty utterance, that has not the backing of sincerity and experience, will be inert and lifeless, and will utterly fail to penetrate and quicken the hearts of men.

The saints and scholars have been eulogising the virtue of peace from the time immemorial, but the world has not been made conflict-free. It seems that "War is the mad game that the world so loves to play." Even the great warrior Napoleon curses war as the "business of the barbarians." But all the talk of history is of nothing almost but fighting and killing and the honour and renown are bestowed on conquerors, who for the most part, are mere butchers of mankind. They even mislead the youth to think that slaughter is the most laudable business of mankind and the most heroic virtues. There are scholars, who not only glorify wars but regard them as pious also. Many a dreadful and long wars have been fought and justified in the name of religion—Jehads, Crusades etc. Supporting wars to end injustices is common but it is also believed that to be prepared for war is one of the most effectual ways of preserving peace. Then there are those who advocate war for human progress and so on. The war against war is going to be no holiday excursion or camping party. The military feelings are too deeply grounded to abdicate their place among our ideals and societal and cultural structures.

Science of war has not only been a part and parcel of our policy but it has been an essential dimension of our educational curriculum also. For example, *Dhanurveda* of Military Science has been recognised as one of the auxiliary scripture (Upaveda) and an essential part of Vedic education. So also in ancient Greece and Rome, training in military warfare is regarded as the most prestigious part of education..

2. Peace-making through Peace-Education

Hence what is required as a precursor of peace-making is introduction of a *Peace-Education* and *Peace-Research*. Before the nuclear era, with the dropping of atom bombs on Hiroshima and Nagasaki, Peace-Education and Peace-Research or war/peace issues, were more or less a fad for the few pacifists. But the unprecedented genocide of the civilian population has caused universal concern. In 1955, Theo Lentz published a book *Towards a Science of Peace*, which tried to point out "the intimate relationship between science and peace"[5] and also scientific methods for conflict-resolution and prevention of war. SIPRI (Stockholm Institute for Peace Research) was set up in Sweden in 1966, which has been publishing *World Armament and Disarmament SIPRI Yearbook* since 1968. By the end of sixties dozens of universities started their peace programmes, peace centres, etc. At present, according to the *Peace Diary, 1995*, we find in the Peace Diary, 1995, a list of *176 International* and *1700 National* organisations working either for Peace-education, Peace-research or Peace-training. More than anything else the nuclear issue is making it essential that peace researchers should do something, as there are more than a dozen nuclear power and also there has been tremendous escalation in their power of devastation and destruction.

The U.S.A. alone possesses about 30,000 nuclear warheads and their power of destruction is thousand times greater than that of atom bomb lashed at Hiroshima. We have almost reached the percept. So when Einstein was asked: "With which weapon shall we fight in the Third World War"?, he replied "I cannot say about the Third War but so far the Fourth War is concerned, we shall be constrained to fight with our *nails* and *teeth*". It means that war has lost its dynamics. It started with *nails* and *teeth* and travelling through ages of stones (Paleolithic and Neolithic Age), sticks and arrows, spears & swords (Metal Age), guns and machine guns (Gun Powder Age) and finally has reached the *Nuclear Age*. But nuclear war will mean the total annihilation of entire mankind. Hence it is compulsion for our survival to explore the "non-violent equivalent of war". It is precisely the reason that inspite of terrific humiliation and staggering losses in men and material, the U.S.A. with 30 thousand nuclear weapons in its possession could not use them in Cuba, Korea, Vietnam, Iraq and Yugoslavia. It means that if we cannot abolish war, war will abolish the whole of humanity and other living beings. There is a choice between "Atom and Ahimsa", Co-existence and Non-existence. Violence is human kinds' enemy number one, whether it is domestic or global, criminal or communal.

3. Our Misconceptions and Scientific Truth

But we still suffer from some worn out orthodoxical beliefs that violence is believed to be ingrained in our inheritance, genetic constitution, behaviour, brain and instinct etc. But in the "Statement of Violence" by the representatives consisting of distinguished anthropologists, psychologists etc. of the *Spanish Unesco* at Seville (Spain) declared on 16-5-86 that it is *scientifically incorrect* to say that :

(1) we have inherited a tendency to make war from our animal ancestors;

(2) that war or any other violent behaviour is *genetically* programmed into our human nature;

(3) that humans have a "violent brain";

(4) that in the course of human evolution there has been a selection for aggressive behaviour; and

(5) that war is caused by 'instinct' or any single motivation.[7]

Hence there is no ground for biological or psychological pessimism. Just as "wars begin in the minds of men, peace also begins in our minds". The same species who invented war is capable of inventing peace.[8] Hence we must cast off our outdated notions that war and violence are not made inevitable by our animal nature.[9] If humanity has to survive, wars must be abolished.

Some learned people do quote that even the Ramayan and the Gita clearly proclaims that in order to fight against unrighteousness, there should be no hesitation to take up arms. But there are two flaws in this argument. Firstly, we have witnessed the saddest tragedy of the war of the Mahabharata. Secondly, there has been qualitative change in the nature of warfare during this nuclear age. Hence we have to explore a "moral equivalent of war" or a "war without violence." It was natural for the ancient science of pedagogy to advocate the study of military science in the system of education as war was an essential part of the then polity.

4. Role of Education in Peace-Making

But now when the war has lost its dynamics, we have to be serious about "peace-education and research" as well as "training for peace and non-violence". Not only this, we must not also neglect "peace extension programmes". Extension is recognised as the third eye of education. The

U.N. rightly calls upon educational institutions and media of mass communication to create the necessary political will. Alexander Pope has said:

"Its education that forms the common mind just as the twig is bent, the toe is inclined". For inculcating the attitude of peace and non-violence, we must have Peace Education or Disarmament Education. The establishment of Peace Education Commission under the auspices of the International Peace Research Association marked a decisive phase in the history of peace-education. The recent contribution and initiative of many western scholars and peace activists in the field of peace-making and peace-research is so amazing that puts Indian scholars, who are supposed to be the traditional custodians of peace and non-violence, to shame. Out of 234 Indian Universities and more than 10 thousand colleges, there exists hardly 10 University Departments and only a dozen colleges having courses in Gandhian Studies and Peace Research.

Hence it is high time to combine the Indian insight and its traditional experience with western peace researches to develop a holistic view of peace-making. It is lack of imagination and creativity that the educational planners in India have failed to realize the importance of introducing peace-science in the scheme of higher education, while incorporating the study of Military Science as an important subject and N.C.C. (Military Training) as extension programmes.

5. Indian Philosophy of History of Peace

There are some reasons. Firstly, in India peace-education has been left to the saints and sages who have invariably emphasized the value of peace throughout their sermons. Secondly, even Indian philosophy and culture are replete with the message of non-violence. Ideology of peace is an integral part of our life and society. We start any important function with the invocation of Peace : "*Om Shanti*" and so we end with "*Om Shanti*". There has been a strong legacy of non-violence in Indian culture. It regards that human society is a ceaseless growth, an unfoldment in terms of spirituality. The Indian philosophy of history believes that man has been steadily progressing towards non-violence or Ahimsa. Our remote ancestors were cannibals. Then they began to live on chase, then of a hunter, then to agriculture and so on. All these are signs of progressive non-violence and diminishing violence. Prophets and *avataras* have also taught the lesson of *ahimsa* more or less. Not one of them has professed to teach *himsa*. Man as animal is violent, but as Spirit is non-violent. And yet violence seem to persist but history and experience are against him. If mankind has steadily progressed towards *ahimsa*, it follows that it has to progress towards it still further.

6. The Holistic Approach

There are generally two approaches of peace-making—Subjective and objective. The subjective approach is generally advocated by the religious seers and sages. According to them, peace does not dwell in outward things, but with the soul; we may preserve it in the midst of the bitterest pain. Five great enemies to peace inhabit with us *viz.* avarice, ambition, envy, anger, and pride. If these enemies were to be banished, we should infallibly enjoy perpetual peace. Hence it is said that if we have not peace within ourselves, it is vain to seek it from outward sources. All our religious teachers emphasize this subjective aspect of peace and prescribe necessary moral discipline and meditational practices. This is known as yoga, which aims at internal peace through the cessation of mental activities. Different schools and religious sects adopt different methods of meditations. There are elements of meditation in almost all religious sects. Some seekers do take on meditation with a purely materialistic outlook for some fulfilment but the core of mediation is spiritual and moral.

This religio-spiritual approach of peace-making is traditional. Saints and sure of all religions have been decrying violence and war and eoulising peace. Blessed are the Peace-makers: for they shall be called children of God" says the Bible[10] (St. Mathew, 5.9). The very word "Islam" means peace. According to Vinoba Bhave, the term Hindu literally means "one who is away from violence". (Hi=Himsa, *i.e.*, violence, +du=away). Their emphasis, however, is upon individual orientation. They think that if we can change the individual, society will be automatically changed. Wars can be abolished or reduced only in direct ration to the abolition or reduction of war-mentality. Moral disarmament must precede physical disarmament. The centre of morality is the individual. Whether it is the doctrine of unity of Mankind, or is unity between science and religion or between religion and religion, it rests on the crest of the individual. Lord Krishna, who had probably more personal experience of war than even a modern Field-Marshal, said long ago: "Lust, Hate, and Greed form the triple gateway into Hell".[11] So they say that the "Paradise is within Thee" as the fount of fragrance is with the musk-deer. Hence the work of the different religions have been very foundational in purifying the very source of fountain. Even in the modern times, the *Inter-religious Federation for World Peace (IRFWP)* and *World Congress of Religion for Peace (WCRP)* or Fellowship in Prayer (FP) and others do try sincerely to achieve peace but it is a tragedy that religion has not always been providing that force of reconciliation across the world today. Instead of providing a constructive force, they have become a destructive forces resulting in a lot of problems.

Organisations like Theosophical Society whose teachings are based on claims of mystic insight into the nature of God and the Laws of the Universe are no doubt making honest endeavour but peace requires a more robust, realistic and holistic approach. Besides, religions are even now plagued with vicious rivalries and a feeling for superiority. Religious approach is one-sided and individualistic. Religious teachers and prophets from the very beginning have been unequivocally dwelling upon peace but it has eluded our grasp so far.

Hence peace demands a supplementary approach which will be more comprehensive, more practical and integral. Although violence has lost its dynamics and scientific basis in the thermo-nuclear age but the hold of violence is so great on our mind that we still put our faith in its capacity to succeed. Hence it requires a multi-pronged attack.

Firstly, we should understand that peace is not only the absence of war, it is much more positive. Even interpreted, the term "non-violence", the Indian equivalent of "peace" (*Ahimsa*) seems to be of negative important form. But it is not so. Non-violence is not only the absence of violence but it implies "active love". Gandhi's great Non-cooperation movement had its root not in hatred, but in love. Hate is the subtlest form of violence.[12] We cannot be non-violent and yet have hate in us.[13] In its positive form, *ahimsa* means the largest love, greatest charity. "If I am a follower of *ahimsa*, I must love my enemy" —says Gandhi.

The second misconception regarding the non-acceptance of non-violence as a viable ideology is that peace is a *passive* and *non-militant* in character. People forget that love is the strongest force the world possesses[14] before which the hardest heart and the grossest ignorance must disappear.[15] Non-violence is not a resignation from all real fighting against wickedness[16], it does not mean meak submission to the will of the evil-doer, but it means the putting of one's whole soul against the will of the tyrant.[17] Gandhi has a distaste for passive spirituality or passive non-violence. He says, "Yours should not merely be a passive spirituality that spends itself in idle meditation, but it should be an active thing which will carry war into the enemy's camp." Giving examples of the militancy of the apostles of peace Gandhi says: "Buddha fearlessly carried the war into the enemy's camp and brought down on its knees an arrogant priesthood. Christ drove out the money-changers from the temple of Jeruselam and drew down curses from the heaven upon the hypocrites and the Pharises".[18] Both were for intensely direct action. Non-violence has no room for cowardice or even weakness.[19] Non-violence and cowardice go ill together.[20] Possession of arms implies an element of fear, if not cowardice. Gandhi's oft quoted statement is inspiring when he says "I would rather have India resort to arms in order to defend her honour than that she should, in cowardly, become or remain a helpless witness to her own dishonour".[21]

The third misconception is that it is a long-drawn out process. But "it is the swiftest the world has seen, for it is the surest".[22] The way of peace insures internal growth and stability.[23] No body questions that the path of non-violence or peace is the nobler way and it prevents brutalization of human nature but there is always a doubt, how a disarmed neutral country can stop external aggression non-violently. Gandhi had suggested some methods of "civilian defence". Firstly it would refuge the passage of invading army by refuging all supplies. Secondly, one should be prepared to re-enact a Thermopylae and should like a living wall of men, women and children inviting the invades to walk over your corpses. Gandhi had shown examples of such courage in the Satyagraha of Bardoli and Peshawar.

It is generally thought that peace and non-violence are cloistered virtues meant only for saints and sages. Gandhi has tried to depict non-violence as a universal principle applicable *in all spheres of life and in all circumstances.* It is applicable in the forum and the legislatures as in the market place.[24] Secondly, it is not mere individual practice but for the practice by groups and communities and nations. This shows its societal and structural dimension.

Some people think that non-violence has no place in politics and wordly affairs. Gandhi has strongly refuted this charge by saying: "I have no use for them as a means of individual salvation".[25]

Peace and non-violence start at home. Domestic violence has become very important these days when children are ill-treated, women abused and even burnt, servants treated like animals and so on. We can teach and practice non-violence even at home. Even toy soldiers should be abolished, "We must disarm the nursery"— said Dr. Paulina Luisi. We must home a temple of peace.

Similarly, we must develop non-violent political science. Dr. Glenn D. Paige has, in his book "To Non-violent Political Science suggested cycles of growth from violence to non-violent awakening, to exploration of non-violent alternatives, and to consolidation of resources in preparation for a new season of work for non-violent global transformation. A centralised political structure is bound to lead to violence and exploitation. Similarly totalitarianism, aggressive nationalism and theocratic fundamentalist states are bound to lead to violence.

Like non-violent politics, we must have Non-violent Economics, which should have a notion of "real progress" and a balanced notion of development. Craze for the growth in material progress, leads to "wrong notion of development" and to the erosion of natural resources and pollution of environment. Gandhi advocated a Economy of Peace and Permanence, appropriate technology and non-exploitative economy.

Violence is also ingrained in our social structure. Our present society must be free from racial, communal, caste and sex discrimination. Discrimination itself is a subtle form of violence. To fight the menace of untouchability or social aparthied, Gandhi put his whole heart and soul for its liquidation. He was a crusader against social injustices like early marriages, oppression of women, casteism, untouchability and so on.

The dream of a peaceful society is impossible without peace-education. The present educational system neglects the education of heart and human values. Secondly it is education of the class rather than the masses. Hence it has become a vested interest. Paule Fairire has therefore advocated the "Pedagogy of the Oppressed". Thirdly, there is a sort of regimentation in the present system, so Evan Ellich has advocated "De-schooling" or "non-formal education". The very concept of competition in class and sports are based on the notion of Darwin's "Struggle for Existence" and "Survival of the Fittest". Education should become an instrument of non-violent social change.

8. Triple Transformation

Peace is no doubt the demand of our time but mere meditation or sermons on peace are not enough. Peace-making needs some new technology and new ideas. Peace is a holistic concept. It is neither subjective alone or objective alone. It is both ideological as well as structural.

With all respects to the teaching of saints and prophets like Mahavira, Buddha, Jesus, Tao, Confucius, Zoraster, Mohammed, Nanak etc., social peace is still elusive. They have emphasised one important point that in order to have a peaceful society, one must have peace of mind and heart. But man does not live in a vacuum but lives in a society. He is product of a social system, which is full of injustices and violence. We cannot think of a moral man in an immoral society. Hence, we have to apply a double edged weapon of reforming the individual and free society from the structural violence. There is of course an important place for mass media and educational apparatus. Thus we dare to suggest a Triangle of Peace-Making through Triple Transformation—(1) Transformation of the individual, (2) Transformation of Society, and (3) Transformation of Education and Media.

9. Organisation of Peace

Organisation is the test of non-violence. In any organisation, there is bound to be some element of coercion and violence. But without organisation, one cannot go ahead. Hence we should evolve such a peace-organisation which must have a sense of dedication. Personal likes and dislikes, ambitions and petty jealousies should have no place here. There should be minimal control. All decisions must be taken with unanimity. They should have living faith in truth and non-violence. Such an organisation is called *Shanti Sena* (Soldiers of Peace).

Therefore, Gandhi said : "Non-violence cannot be preached. It has to be practised". The practice of violence can be taught to people by outward symbols. We shoot at boards, then at targets, then at beasts. Then we are passed as experts in the art of destruction. The non-violent mass has no outward weapon, therefore, not only his speech out his action also seems ineffective..... Non-violence when it becomes active, travels with extraordinary velocity and then it becomes a miracle. Hence what is necessary today is the organisation of non-violence. For this Gandhi had mooted the idea of the formation of Shanti Sena (Peace Corps) ultimately forming a Peace Brigade. The War Resistors International at its conference at Wardha in 1960, had an International Shanti Sena under Mr. A.J. Masts while Michael Scott and Jaya Prakash Narayan were chosen to lead the European and Asian units respectively. Dr. G. Ram Chandran, a close disciple of Gandhi and the founder Vice-Chancellor of Gandhigram Rural University (near Madurai in South India), started Shanti Sena centre as educational experiment. Instead of having the usual unit of para-military outfit National Cadet Corpse (N.C.C.), Mr. Ram Chandran had the courage to set up Shanti Sena training programme as an Extension activity in his University, which was very successful for sometime. Pt. Nehru addressing the rally of Gandhi Gram Shanti Sena, had said; "Our fight against violence and hatred will have no meaning if we are not ready to involve the youths. Every student of this country should become a messenger of peace."

Martin Luther King (Jr.) taking the salute of Santi Sena said, "India has great potentials and the concept of peace army is spreading. It is bound to grow as it holds out great promise to the entire humanity. Perhaps this alone will put us back from the percipice." Prof. Glenn Paige (Hawii) said, " The future of mankind is not certainly in the hands of soldiers of the army, but in the hands of the Shanti Sainiks who are to create a new social order. He further said: "The Shanti Sena of the Gandhigram University is a practical vision of a warless society, a paradigm of practical living." The veteran non-violent man of this sub-continent only next to Gandhi and who had floated *Khudai Khidmatgar* (Servants of God) on the pattern of Khan Abdul Gaffar Khan who had visited Gandhigram and witnessed the rally of Shanti Sena, he exclaimed: "My eyes water when I see you. You are the real children of God".[26] The former U.S. Ambassador to India, Robert Goheen in his convocation address to the G.R.I. said: "While the rest of the world is engaged in a serious bid to evolve non-violent alternatives I see in Gandhigram a model for the rest of the university."

The idea of organisation of Peace Force had originally struck Gandhi as a substitute for police and para-military force to control problems of civilian and communal conflicts. He had not only prepared its pledge but also a blue-print of its organisation. The Seven Commandments which Gandhi had prescribed for the Shanti Sainiks are crucial to understand its organisational philosophy[29]:

1. A Shanti Sainik must have living faith in non-violence, which is impossible without a faith in God.
2. He/She must have an equal regard for all religions.
3. He/She will cultivate love of the people through selfless service.
4. He/She will do peace work singly or in groups.
5. He/She must have a character beyond reproach and known for his strict impartiality.
6. He/She will not wait till the conflagration breaks out, but will try to handle the situation in anticipation.
7. There should be a distinctive dress.

The membership, in its very nature of a movement like Shanti-Sena cannot be large. Every member of the

Shanti-Sena has to take a pledge and undergo a strict training. The pledge is assertion of one's resolve:

1. To work of peace and be prepared, if need be to lay down my life for it;
2. To do best to rise above the distinctions of caste, sect, colour, and party because they deny the unity of man;
3. Not to take part in any war;
4. To help in creating means and conditions of non-violent defence;
5. To develop regularly a part of my time to service of my fellowmen; and
6. Accept the discipline of Shanti Sena.[30]

Gandhi did not only preach about Shanti Sena he also lived and died like a Shanti Sena. He was aware of social and cultural diversities in India having the potentials of occassional conflicts and tension. Besides, he had a long range view about the threat to democracy in case three is ascendancy of military power over the civil power, which he wrote in his Last Testament.[31] Gandhi had more than once staked his life to control the communal riots. He was able to stop the mass insanity with his presence—something the entire military might of India and Pakistan failed to achieve. This promoted the then Governor-General of India, Earl Mountbatton to call Gandhi, "the one-man Boundary Commission". He had visited the worst riot affected areas of Noakhali, Bihar and Delhi and was planning to visit Pakistan. But he fell to the bullets of the assassin. As a commander of Shanti Sena, he gave the command and as a Shanti Sainik he laid his life as a martyr of peace. After the death of Mahatma Gandhi, Acharya Vinoba Bhave, his spiritual disciple, took the reigns of Shanti Sena and gave wider dimension — "Peace is mind and revolution in the mode of society".[32] According to him, the person having peace in mind has so much capability of revolutionising the mode of society. Thus he saw a deep inherent relation between internal peace and external revolution. So also Jaya Prakash Narayan also look initiative for restoration of peace at many places in India. It was he who encouraged some 400 dacoits of Chambal area to surrender their arms and resolved to lead a new life. Dr. G. Ramchandran, another disciple of Gandhi must be credited with introducing the Shanti Sena training programme in the Gandhigram Rural University as an instrument of peace-building. Narayan Desai, who worked with Jaya Prakash Narayan as Secretary of All India Shanti Sena Mandal. He established a centre of Peace Training at Bedchi in Gujrat. An outfit for the training of peace volunteer has also be floated with the name of Ahimsa-Vahini.

9. Epilogue

The western scholars like Gene Sharp, Johan, Galtung, Gleen D. Paige etc. must be credited with pioneering peace studies. Johan Galtung is one of the founders of modern piece studies having founded the first International Peace Research Institute in Oslo and co-founded the International Peace Research Association and launching the Journal of Peace Research. He has taught at 50 universities and published more than 80 books on peace studies. He appreciated Gandhi's taking up the case of structural violence with non-violent revolution. He considers Gandhian model of Satyagraha as a "moral equivalent of war". "True heroism is not killing, it is risking one's own life to prevent killing." Gene Sharp's advocacy of "civilian based defence policy" is a great contribution in peace-making. Prof. Gleen Paige is a champion of Non-violent International Order and an ardent advocate of Non-violent Political Science. Incidentally all these three peace-stalwarts of the west are deeply inspired by Gandhi. So far great western Peace-activists like Martin Luther King, Petra Kelly and Eastern Peace-thinkers and activists like Daisaku Ikida of Japan and A.T. Ariyaratne of Sri Lanka acknowledge frankly their source of inspiration of Gandhi.

This explains that Gandhi's idea of Peace-making is holistic and more practical. Gandhi's approach to life is rational. To him life is a unity. It cannot be divided into watertight compartments called spiritual and material. He was not a visionary but a practical idealist. To him, the religion of non-violence is not meant only for the *Rishis* and *saints*, it is meant for the common people as well. As we come close to the dawn of the 21st century, we come to realize that the Gandhian perspective peace-making finds greater acceptance. His was the first experiment of systematic non-violent resistance in the social sphere. He believes in "Spirituality in Action". His non-violence is not based on any theoretical assumption and utopian sentimental vision. It was composite and total. He lived every inch of what he professed. Peace was not his ritual, it was his life.

REFERENCES

1. Gandhi, M.K., *Harijan*, 28.1.39.
2. *Ibid., Harijan*, 8.6.35.
3. *Ibid., Young India*, 11.8.1927.
4. *Ibid., Young India*, 11.8.1927.
5. Lentz, Theo, Towards a Science of Peace, New York: Bookman Associates, 1955, p.V.
6. Peace Diary and World Peace Directory, 1955, London XII 9DX, Housemans Peace Research Project, ed. Albert Beale, 1995.

7. Seville, "State on Violence", 16.5.1986.

8. *Ibid.*

9. Paige, Gleen, To Non-violent Political Science, Honolulu: University of Hawaii, 1993, p. 139.

10. New Testament, St. Mathew, 5.9.

11. *Gita,* 17.21.

12. Gandhi, M.K., *Young India,* 6.8.25.

13. Gandhi, M.K., *Harijan,* 17.8.34.

14. Gandhi, M.K., *Young India,* 19.2.25.

15. Gandhi, M.K., *Young India,* 19.2.25.

16. *Ibid., Young India,* 8.10.25.

17. *Ibid., Young India,* 11.8.20.

18. *Ibid., Young India,* 12.5.20.

19. *Ibid., Young India,* 16.6.27.

20. *Ibid., Young India,* 18.12.24.

21. *Ibid., Young India,* 11.8.20.

22. *Ibid., Young India,* 30.4.45.

23. *Ibid., Young India,* 20.5.26.

24. Gandhi, M.K., *Harijan,* 8.5.37.

25. Gandhi, M.K., *Amrit Bazar Patrika,* 30.6.44.

26. Radhakrishnan, N.(ed.) Gandhi and Youth: The Shanti Sena of GRI, Gandhigram : 1989, pp. 40-43.

27. Quoted in Bhartiya Shanti Sena, Paunar, 1982, p. 5.

28. Gandhi, M.K., Quoted in Gandhian Non-violence: A Trainer's Manual, N. Radhakrishnan, New Delhi: Gandhi Smrti & Darshan, 1997, p. 24.

29. *Ibid.*, p. 19; Gandhi and Youth, pp. 8/9.
30. *Ibid.*, p. 9, Gandhi and Youth, pp. 15-16.
31. Gandhi, M.K., *Harijan Sevak*, 8.2.48 (The Last Public document released on 30th Jan., 1948 to the Secretary to the Indian National Congress).
32. Bhartiya Shanti Sena, p. 51.

Chapter 4

EDUCATION FOR PEACE

Education in military science is as old as the human history. Even in India, a traditional land of peace and non-violence, science of warfare called *Dhanurveda* was recognised as an essential part of the Vedic education. Perhaps it was left to the individual saints and sages like Patanjali, Mahavira and Buddha to carry the lessons in peace through informal system of education contained in their sermons. Fighting war, as if, have been a part of our social and civilizational life. The evolutionary history shows that we started fighting with our teeth and nails, then with stones in the Paleolithic and Neolethic Ages, then with spears and swords etc. in the Metal age, and then with guns, machine guns, bombs etc. But now we have entered into Atomic Age in which we have developed unlimited power of destruction. The U.S.A. alone possess atleast 30000 dreadful hydrogen bombs before which Hiroshima and Nagasaki bombs fade into insignificance. Then there are other nuclear powers also. This has changed the very character of war. Virtually war has lost it dynamics as any atomic war can wipe out the entire human and animal existence. The world "now stands on the brink of the final abyss."

Before the dropping of atom bombs on the twin cities of Japan, the question of Peace-education or Peace-Research or war/peace issue, were more or less in exclusive fad of a few pacifists. But the experience of atom bomb made war everybody's concern. Even the first world war had already proved the futility of waging a war to stop all wars. It was only a sentimental dream. With this new experience of the atom bomb, it was finally established that if a third world war took place it would be a total disaster for life as a whole on this planet. So when somebody asked Einstin, with which weapon shall be fight the third war, he said : "I cannot say about the third war, but we shall definitely fight the Fourth war with our teeth and nails like our primitive fathers." It was precisely the reason why U.S.A. inspite of having 30 thousands nuclear warheads could not use them in Cuba, Korea, Veitnam, Iraq and Yogoslavia although it suffered unprecedented humiliation and physical losses. Now there are more than 1000 peace Research Education Centres of Institutes in the west. In India, the Education Commission (1964-66) Report in the very first chapter has posed a challenging alternative to choose between "Atom and Ahimsa" with a warning of rating down a nuclear abyss to ruin and annihilation. However, the perspective paper of the Government fails to provide even a distant suggestion for the introduction of Peace Education in the formal curriculum of our Universities. Perhaps the Indian scholars have not paid enough attention to some of the efforts and initiative for peace which should have been forthcoming from them by virtue of rich tradition of peace which India has given to the world. Perhaps we also forget that violence is human kinds enemy, whether it is international or domestic field. Violence does not only bring a bad image to our nation, it also weakens the very fabric of our society and the nation. Unfortunately, violence is becoming a way of life. Politicalisation of criminals and criminalisation of politics is a threat to our civic life. It seems that we have become more Darwinians in implementing the doctrine of struggle for Existence and bad Marxians in perpetuating blood-bath either in the name of religion, or caste or language instead of class-struggle. Even campus violence has forced the Vice-Chancellors to maintain a strong and regular contingent of security force. We cannot hold examinations or celebrate our religious festivals or Pujas without assistance of para-military forces. This is a very dangerous omen for the survival of democracy. Gandhi in his last testament has rightly warned against the usurption of civic powers by military or semi-military power. We have witnessed the gradual eclipse of democratic systems in many Asian and African countries, especially between Jakarta to Cairo. Besides, the cost of military, para-military or military put a great burden on the ordinary citizens. Total military expenditure of the world is over 800 billion dollars per annum. Expenses on para-military forces to control the internal disturbances have risen atleast 500 times from the time of British withdrawal. We have developed a culture of violence, which is essential to the growth of creativity and goodness. In India some people are very prompt to quote that even the Ramayan and the Gita teaches that in order to right against unrighteousness, we should not hesitate to take up arms. First of all, the ultimate result of the Mahabharata is dreadful. Today, the atomic war would be more and more dreadful than the Mahabharata. It means that situations have qualitatively changed. Hence, we have to evolve a "moral equivalent" or "a non-violent alternative" of war and fighting injustice. Total disarmament is no doubt a far cry but perhaps there is no alternative because we have to choose between "co-existence and non-existence", between disarmament and destruction. The Final Document of U.N. Assembly Session on Disarmament (23rd May to 1st July 1978) calls upon all the people of the world to end the "colossal waste of resources" on militarization that brings physical insecurity, economic deprivation and cultural disintegration. It is more tragic to see atleast half of the fellow beings of our globe ill-fed, ill-clad and sunk into ill-health and illiteracy and spend the precious resources to produce the arsenals of destruction. The U.N. also calls upon educational institutions and media of mass communication to create the political will because,

"It is education that forms the common mind just as the twin the tree's inclined" - Alexander Pope. For this we urgently need 'Disarmament Education' or Peace Education accompanied by seminars, dialogues, adult education programmes. The establishment of the Peace Education Commission under the auspices of the International Peace Research Association marked a decisive phase in the history of peace education. The recent contribution and initiative of western thinkers in the field of peace-research is so amazing that puts Indians as traditional custodians of peace and non-violence to shame. Hence this is high time that we must endeavour to combine the Indian insight and faith with the zeal and tenacity of western peace researchers and activists to build a defence of peace. We must remember the inspiring optimism of the UNSCO's declaration. "Since wars begin in the minds of men, it is in the minds of men that the defence of peace must be constructed."

It is singular lack of imagination and creativity that the educational planners have failed to realise the importance of introducing Peace-Education, Peace-Research, Peace-Training and Peace work as extension programme in the Universities while incorporating the study of Military Science as an important subject and N.C.C. as extension programme. We forget that the youth trained in non-violence will be the best guarantee to world peace. Pt. Jawaharlal Nehru while taking the salute from the volunteers of Santi Seva at Ganghigram had also admitted : "Our fight against violence and hatred will have no meaning if we are not ready to involve the youths in educating the masses. Every student of this country should be trained in non-violence. "Martin Luther King (Jr) was so much impressed with the concept of Peace Army (Santi Sena) that he said: "Perhaps this alone will pull back from the percipice". "The future of mankind is not certainly in the hands of the soldiers of the army, but in the hands of the Santi Sainiks"- says Professor Glenn D. Paige. To think that the power of state alone is the guarantee for our peace and security is not only a delusion, it is self-defeatism par excellence and an insult to the collective conscience of mankind. Hence it is necessary to explore the cultural power and cultural dynamics so that we can meet the challenges and abbretions in man's nature. Santi Seva is therefore the cultural equivalent of bruse power of the State. A non-violent paradigm shift is necessary in education, as "we are machines, second hand people. We are the result of thousands of years propaganda" (J. Krishnamurty, *Beyond Violence*, New York: Harper Row, 1970, p. 138). Violence has no doubt lost its dynamics, people are fed up with violence, but non-violence has not taken the root because violence is rooted in our mental disperitions from the time immemorial. Peace demands a new desire, a new asceticism and a new habit and response. It is due to our cynicism that we still do not believe that "the law of love is the single tool for solving conflict. But our difficulty is that we do not find any visible sanction behind Santi Seva or a 'Soldiers of Peace', like the one of state structure behind the each. Vinoba suggests a moral authority behind Santi Seva in the form of a continuous selfless service and public contact. There are atleast 13 countries in the world today that have *no army* and there are another 12 countries that have no army but have only defence Treaty with another country. There are 31 countries that recognise conscientious objection to

Military Service. With the establishment of European Parliament, European Market and so on, individuals countries have been giving up their claims of keeping army, which has become a heavily costly affairs.

Although violence has lost its ground during this thermonuclear age but the hold of violence is so great that even though it has failed a thousand times, we still put faith in its capacity to succeed, as it is rooted in our mental dispositions. It might be that we have inherited it from the animals, our immediate predecessor in the scheme of evolution. Hence we need a mind which is free from its own conditioning. Hence, during the very ancient time, there had been provision for the study of military science but so far peace-science was concerned, it was left to the spiritual seers and religious saints to propagate the virtues of peace. We have spent colossal amount of time and resources to perfect the instruments of destruction, now it is high time to explore the power of non-violence, conflict-resolution and Santi Seva. We should understand what is peace? Peace is not only the absence of war. It is a holistic concept. It involves both the ideology of peace and peace in the structure of society. Gandhian concept of peace is neither *utopian* nor simply *ethico-spiritual* but also *structural* and integral. It is not only subjective but also objective. Though Gandhi also believes that if we have not peace within ourselves, it is vain to seek it from outward sources but he does not neglect the societal and objective factors of peace. So while emphasising the need of non-absolution in thought leading to intellectual tolerance, faith in essential goodness of man, change of heart and other ethical-spiritual conditions, he equally stresses to develop a culture of non-violence. He went beyond the personalistic and ethico-religious approach and exposed that the problem of war/peace is rooted in the way civilizational structure—in its technology, polity economics and the last but not the least in its pedagogical frame.

So far Economics of Peace is concerned, Gandhi came to the conclusion that it is based on a false notion of 'Progress'. With the wrong notion of 'Progress', we have a 'wrong notion ·of development'. The club of Rome Report says "In many (third world) countries two decades of development have produced meagre results include for about two thirds of humanity the increase in per capita income has been less than one dollar a year for the last twenty years. Even this increase, miserable it may seem has been unevenly distributed, with poorest 40% of population hopelessly squeezed in the struggle for existence and sometimes getting even less than is received almost a quarter of century ago. The U.S.A. with 6% of world population consumes about 40% of world resources. Hence unless we develop in rational view of *progress* we cannot have an appropriate development and consequences appropriate technology. The prosperity of western nations is mostly a story of exploitation of developing nations of Asia and Africa through the technique of industrialisation which inevitably leads to centralisation and that cannot be sustained and defended without adequate force. Hence militarization is inherent in this system. Hence Gandhi advocated an Economy of peace, sustainable development, and technology with human face.

Similarly, we have inherited a model of violent state. The state, rather than *man* has become the measure of political progress. Even the democratic state has become like a Livathan. Modern technology and media have made the state almost omnipotent. Hence Gandhi wanted to usher a politics of peace and individual freedom. Gandhi believed with Thoreau in the doctrine of the "Least Government" that government is the best which governs the least." With the enormous increase in the "size and powers of the modern State, the individuals feels like a mere cog in a huge machine. The State represents violence in a concentrated and organised form. Hence, if we want a policy of peace, we have to develop a new polity based on democratic decentralisation, participatory democracy, and goodness politics. Real democracy and violence can ill go together Politics of peace is also in conflict with rational chauvinism or religious fundamentalism. Gandhi has always looked on the whole of humanity as one. God never made these frontiers and a new world society should be our ideal.

Like politics and economics of peace, we must try to free our society from racial, communal, caste and sex discrimination itself is a subtle form of violence. We must say 'no' to the 'religious manicas' and uphold the ideal of *Sarvadharma-sambhava* on universal religion. Gandhi fought the most fiercely but non-violently the battle against aparthied both in Africa and India. In fact, social peace is a precondition of world peace.

Lastly, comes education, though it is not the last in matter of importance. What sculpture is to a piece of marble, education is to the human soul. We have a conflict-ridden and violence-prone society because we do not have peace-education in our system. The violence of formal education is subtle but dangerous. The present educational system creates a class, it is a vested interest and it cannot become an instrument of peace. Hence Evan Illich has advocated "De-schooling" or "non-formal education" and Paul Frauire has put before us a strong case of the Pedagogy of the Oppressed". Hence unless we remove the structure violence in the very system of education, we cannot hope to make it an instrument of peace and social change.

Conclusion

Peace is no doubt the demand of our time but we must develop an appropriate technology of peace-making. Any isolated approach would not be fruitful. Life is a unity and hence we cannot divide it into watertight compartments-subjective and objective, political and social, ideological and structural. We cannot afford to neglect the selfless teachings of religious saints like Socrates, Mahavira, Buddha, Jesus, Tao, Mohamed etc. to cultivate peace of mind. They have been carrying the torch of peace since time immemorial but with utmost humility we must say that it is not enough. We must try to go into the very structure of society where violence is present in subtle forms.

But from where should we begin? There is violence in politics, economics, social system, religion etc. Even education has become a vested interest. But amidst encircling gloom, education is the last hope of humanity. It is through peace-education that our mental attitude can change. We have spent enormous resources to perfect the weapons of war. If we could spend the smallest part of our time and resources on Peace-education, there can be a Kingdom of God on Earth. Science and scientific knowledge his made us arrogant and often sinister. Science needs spirituality as its guide to save this world from impending catastrophy. Gandhi did not only gave us the theory of peace but has demonstrated the efficacy of peace through Satyagraha and Santi Sena. Let us supplement his exploration and even correct where he is wrong or inadequate. Peace is no monopoly of Gandhi.

Chapter 5

NUCLEAR INDIA

Indeed it was unique forecast of the "Organise (No. 42) just a week before the atomic blasts under front page title- *Nuclear India*. It was strange coincidence that R.S.S. Chief Professor Rajendra Singh (Rajju Bhaiya) had visited Bhabha Atomic Research Institute at that every time. An information which could not be divulged to the Cabinet for security reasons and the Kite-like penetrating eyes of C.I.A. and Pentagon could not detect in advance, the R.S.S.-B.J.P. Chief English Organ could have some inkling as to bring out a special number on "Nuclear India". This quite fits in with the B.J.P. manifesto and B.J.P. agenda. I only wish that they should have done it more openly and boldly. But after the tests, the poor Prime Minister was constrained to shift his stand and statement atleast nine times and perhaps the Govt. stand is not still clear as to the necessity of these blasts. It is understand that popular sentiment in both the countries are in favour of these blasts. Just after the five Indian blast, a Survey conducted revealed that 91.7% people supported these tests and 82% people were in favour of India making the bomb. But gradually these sentiments have been subsiding. In the beginning, there was hardly any clear protest from any quarters. Even Sarvodaya workers could not organise even a symbolic protest. But now, things are otherwise. Just yesterday a report appeared in the Press that a strong batch of 1000 Punjabis & Sikhs will march in protest on the streets of Delhi as in case of nuclear confrontation between India and Pakistan, Punjab will be the most vulnerable sight of devastation. We should remember that Punjabis have been the best warriors of India and at present there is political collaboration between the BJP and the Akalis. This is the imperative of the situation. It has nothing to do either with courage or cowardice.

I have failed to grasp the clear motivations of these tests from national and international considerations. Let me analyse :

(a) The most vocal but equally vague argument in favour of these blasts is the *national security*. Mr. I.K.Gujral, the former Prime Minister of India rightly challenged that there was no perception of any immediate danger to our national security. The Govt. has not been able to contradict it. This means that in the immediate future, there was no danger to security. Hence its chorus might play on the sentiments of the people but it has nothing to do with the reality.

(b) Suppose, there was danger to national security, it is not clear that simply tests would counter it. There is always a gap between the tests and making the bomb and providing strategic carreer etc. Hence these tests without the will to make the bomb is an useless exercise. The Prime Minister is on record to say that India will not make the bomb. Either he does not mean what he says or he says that he does not mean. The basic feature of pose-Pokhran international diplomacy by India is to convince the world opinion that India is not in favour of manufacturing atom bomb and it wants a nuclear arsenal free world.

(c) Suppose India could acquire nuclear capability

but there the question arises, will it use and against whom? India's Defence Minister has openly but headlessly declared that China is its enemy number one but according to the BJP leaders, it is Pakistan. Whatever might be the truth, Pakistan has also developed nuclear power as revealed in five blasts just after the Indian blasts. From the recent report, China has helped Pakistan with rare materials and technical know how, Iran and Saudi Arabia and some other Islamic States have helped with money. China's nuclear capability are well known. Even politically, how dangerous it is to let two antagonists come together? Any way, any atomic attach from India either on Pakistan or China will not be in its own advantage, rather their mixed might together with clandestine support of the U.S.A. will prove practically more dangerous. The conclusion is that nuclear war between India-Pak-China is an impossibility. What to speak of India and Pakistan, even U.S.A. with a stockpiles of about 30,000 nuclear war-heads after effecting more than 1200 blasts could not use atom bomb even where it got humiliated and extremely taxed in case of Cuban crisis, Korean and Vietnam wars, it could not dare to use nuclear weapons after its first use in Hiroshima/Nagasaki in 1945, to think that India can use it is an unhealthy illusion.

(d) Hence everybody knows that ***atom bomb*** cannot be used but then might be said that it was a mere *"show of strength and power"*, as Dr. Murli Manohar Joshi, a strongman of B.J.P. declared just after the tests. How silly it looked when Pakistan also showed its strength? Such argument are not deserved from such responsible man. In the

present world military intelligence gives all such informations. Hence just to demonstrate own's power, our need not indulge into such counter-productive ventures.

(e) There is another argument in favour that now India will join Nuclear Club. Both President Clinton and Madame Albright have categorically said that Indian cannot become its member as only these countries which joined before 1967 were illigible. In Security Council, U.S.A., U.K., China and France have sided together. Even Russia is very much disappointed and sore. Hence it was a miscalculation on the part of India to earn the right of membership of the Nuclear Club.

(f) In international politics, India has never been isolated as today. Even friendly Japan, Australia and many other countries have been hurt. The wild reactions are apparent. The Security Council condemned India's action unanimously. So is the response of G-7 and other such groups. It seems that India has lost all the reuse capital of being a peaceful country. What India could not suffer even opposing U.S.A. on the recognition of Chinese issue, has suffered now. It is a moral backlash. There has been never so much caricatures of India's advocacy of peace non-violence and its legacy of Buddha, Mahavira and Gandhi. Hence this has affected our capacity of cultural leadership. Now to get a seat in the U.N.O. has become more difficult.

(g) Apart from moral and cultural costs for these blasts, we have heavily paid the economic costs in the form of international sanctions. Dr. Raja Ramanna has said that it requires atleast Rs. 3000

crores to induct atomic weapons the use of military, which Indian economy cannot bear. We have the lessons of military-oriented economy of U.S.S.R. which has resulted in such economic catastrophy. India is a poor country. There are 61% people living below the poverty line and atleast 50% people are illiterate. There is a heavy foreign debt and more than one fourth of our national revenue goes to pay the interest. If we increase our Defence budget axe will tall on social service items like education, health etc. Inspite of the great military power of Chiang-Ki-Shek or U.S.S.R. They crumbled because of internal weaknesses. India should take lessons from them.

(h) There is an outdated argument of deterrance. It is said that India possesses nuclear weapons will deter others to cast an evil eye upon it. As nuclears weapons of any country are not for use and like India. Its main adverse in Pakistan and China are also nuclear powers the argument of deterrence is meaningless. Even when military almight is assessed today, it is done is twins of conventional army and weapons. Even after atomic war between two nations, conventional army will have it role. Hence under present nuclear non-monopoly atomic deterrance is not practical.

(i) Lastly, as Swami Vivekanand has said that every nation has its own mission and tradition. Nations are not formed in a day, the formation requires years. No country can become a nation by producing a race of immitators. Violent nationalism and playing on the cheap sentiments of the people are the royal road to dictatorship and imperialism. I can understand the political compulsions of the B.J.P. but the compulsions of

> India's culture is greater. One should not try to play with it. Growing internationalisation of the Kashmir issue and isolation of India in world community and U.S.-China-Pak nexus are some of the net losses of there blasts of bravodo. I am not in favour of distablizing the Govt. but let them not distablize the national legacy of people and non-violence.

Every nation or country has a mission of its own. Then there are its traditions which are built in the long process of history. Non-violence and peace has been declared our supreme virtue. (*Ahimsa Parma Dharmah*) A war hysteria is being whipped. The tragedy is that the peace-loving Indian nation is going the wrong way. From the report of a new paper survey, 91.7% people had supported the atomic tests and 82% people were in favour of India making the Bomb. However, initial gusto soon subsided and there has been sustained and effective protests against this trend. Nearly one thousand Punjabi Sikhs has chosen to come on the street is protest against nuclear preparation as they think that in case of Indo-Pak war, they will suffer most.

The international pressure has benumbed India and the Indian Prime Minister has told the U.N.O. that now onwards it will have no tests and has also declared "no first attack". This is the result of somewhat confused thinking. If it is not to be tested further, why then went for it. Beker was the Nehru doctrine of non-making bomb nor signing the C.T.B.T. because it was openly discriminating and it went in favour of big powers. But now India is in a contradicting position and it has not got any benefit also. China has taken retaliatory positions, Pakistan already exploded its own bomb. So India has lost its moral leadership in the world without getting any practical benefits.

Nuclear weapons and nuclear projects is neither accident free nor safe. The incident of chernoybel and some other such sites. The waste from Atomic reactors have been poring serious dangers. Viewing all these difficulties, many peace-activists have launched strong protests. A young man Sri Sandeep Pandey has successfully completed a Protests March from Pokhran to Sarnath. It has been widely welcomed. The international opinion is also against nuclearisation of India. The deadlock between Indian-Pak dialogue must end peace talks should start.

It is sariligious to associate the names of Buddha or Gandhi is support of having atom bomb. When the tests had occured, the code word was "Buddha Smiles". This is culturally reprehensible. Buddha or Gandhi are symbols of peace and compassion. Gandhi is on record to decry the manufacture of atom bomb. Hence to say that had Gandhi been alive, he would have blessed it, is the greatest insult to Gandhi. Gandhi was against all teams of violence, what to speak of atom bomb. Science of war leads to dictatorship pure and simple. Gandhi had invented the 'moral equivalent of war' in the form of Satyagraha.

Chapter 6

THE GANDHIAN HIMALAYAN POLICY

Himalaya is not only a splendid chain of mountains, it is also a symbol of unity of man and nature. In Indian ethos, entire cosmos is a unity between human beings, lower animals, vegetable kingdom and the material world. Hence whether there are mountains or rivers, earth or sky they are looked at with veneration. This may look little out of date today but such a "reverence for the earth" and other elements are necessary when we have been receiving deadly warnings from the ecological horizons. We have cut down the forests and thereby invited flood havoc. With the change of climate, and "the rape of the earth" etc. have compelled us to think of inventing renewable sources of energy and sustainable development. The depletion of resources, the holes in the ozone layers, acid rains, nuclear winter and threatening water scarcity are some of the danger-signals and the "price of progress".

1. Geographical Dimension

The entire 2400 Km long Himalayan mountain arc continues to be built up by an unceasing succession of catastrophic over—thrusting, creating once every few hundred years a series of great earthquakes (m 8.5) from one end to the other. The steady source of stress required to sustain this process is provided by the persistent northward drive of the strong Indian plate against the thickened and now fortified butresses of the Tibetan plateau. As a result, the whole Indian continent is at any given time, under high stress particularly its northern limb which penetrates unabatedly into the rest of Asia.

The mounting internal stresses may create giant leap of about 6 to 10 or perhaps 20 metres. In short dynamic setting of the Himalayas, its uniformity of deformal style from east to west, uniform north-south conversion of the two continents astride the Himalayan arc requires with the recurrents time and years or horrible pointers to create earthquakes. The Himalayan mountain arc, is segmented by tear faults ripped by strong continental grains of the underthrusting Indian plateau, which happen to be parallel or sub-parallel to the direction of slip. It should thus be clear that earthquake hazards all along the Himalaya which marks the world's most active locus of continental convergence earthquakes, is generally quite high.

Forests serve as the defensive shield of the mountains but our greed has led cutting down the trees for money with the result that there has been great erosion of the Himalayas creating high bed of the rivers inviting flood and other havocs. Hence, all along range scientific consideration based on geographical and total ecological aspects have to be taken into account for enunciating a Himalayan policy. The whole of Himalayan problem should be seen from regional point of view and a meeting should be organised of the all the Himalayan countries like China, India, Pakistan, Nepal, Bhutan, Bangladesh, Burma etc. in order to establish "a Save the Himalaya Movement". Voluntary organisation in Europe and elsewhere should co-operate not to exploit this region in a cruel commercial manner.

2. Political Dimension

Whatever may be the cultural history of the Himalayas *vis-a-vis* India we should think that Himalaya is the common property of all the Himalayan countries and not the monopoly of India. It is a tragedy that the Himalayan countries have been victims of internal as well as external stresses and strains. Then there are inter-state problems due to rivers and land locked status of some of the countries. Himalaya no longer is the sentry of India nevertheless Himalayan boundary of India is in turmoil from Kashmir to North-East. Himalayan states have been facing worst insurgency with outside support. Therefore for a long term Himalayan policy it is more necessary to evolve a two fold programme of close relationship with the Himalayan neighbours as well as evolving an internal policy which can meet the aspirations of the people, the regional imbalances and the neglect of Himalayan region have to be rectified and a strong package programme has to be introduced.

3. Economic Dimension

It is a tragedy that though the Himalayan region is the most rich region in natural resources, the people are in a state of utter poverty and miseries. Because of climatic conditions people have healthy body but they are reeling under poverty. The big contractors and timber merchants have only one point programme of exploitation of its natural resources. Due to cutting of forests there has been severe problem of water scarcity and getting livelihood through forests. The local cottage industries have been ruined. Multinationals have steadly crept into this region and they purchase all their fruits and vegetables at cheap price. They also introduce wine among these unsophisticated people. With the result that they became poor and poorer. Economic development converts everything into cash and money becomes the Supreme God.

Conclusion

It is a sad commentary on our part not to have evolved a comprehensive Himalayan policy taking its ecological, political and economic dimensions. The dynamic nature of Himalayan geology and its ecological chastity must be taken into consideration. The present development model aim to bring big dams and big projects. There should some organisations like SAARC or ASEAN for the Himalayan region. There should be a Himalayan fraternity or Himalayan brotherhood to tackle multi dimensional problems of Himalaya's. It cannot be a sectarian problem, in fact it is a human problem.

Chapter 7

FREEDOM THROUGH NON-VIOLENCE

'In the golden age of Asia, Korea was one of its lamp-bearers and that Lamp is waiting to be delighted again, for the illumination of the East".[1]

These are the words from Indian Nobel Laurete R.N. Tagore, who epitomized the Indian spirituality, thought, literature and art. Although politically detached, he always protested against injustice as a matter of moral duty. He inspired the humankind to resist the force of colonialism. Whether in India or Korea. Korea, then under the Japanese colonial rule looked forward to such inspirations and had invited Tagore to visit their country. Though Tagore could not visit Korea then, he was deeply moved by the invitation extended to him through Korean patriotic feelings which found expression in the poem.[2] Not only this he supported the Korean cause even in front of a crowd in Japan in 1924, notwithstanding the protocol. As the Poet had led an agitation against the partition of Bengal by the then colonial powers and had surrendered his knighthood when he heard of the brutal killings of hundreds of innocent and peaceful Indians at Jallianwala Bagh in Punjab, so Tagore had sympathised with the Korean non-violent mass resistance as a human being. What had been expressed on the surface, might have been like the tip of the iceberg of his deep anguish and agony and fierce anger that lay in his heart.

There is a marked similarly between Korean and Indian struggle of Independence. Just as the Japanese ruthlessly attempted to suppress Korean nationalism whenever it appeared and thousands were killed and imprisoned in the first three years after annexation in 1910, and there were 70 separate encounters between Korean patriot-insurgents and Japanese authorities, similarly in India as early as in 1857, an armed revolt called the First War of Indian Independence was started to end the political domination and economic exploitation by the British colonialists. But unfortunately, because of multiple factors, the battle was lost. Repression and oppression reached their climax. Then it was challenged by innumerable freedom-fighters courting life-imprisonment and facing gallows. A desire to resist oppression is implemented in the nature of man. While moderate section adopted the constitutional methods of prayer, petition and delegations, the fire-brand youngmen, like the chivalosous Koreans took to insurgency terrorism etc. to fight the colonial rule. However, when Gandhi assumed the leadership after his return from South Africa, where he had fought a crucial non-violent fight against racial discrimination under the garb of colonialism, the mainstream of Indian Freedom Movement assumed a peaceful, non-violent but powerful mass-character. The nationalism of colonial peoples that followed World War I had its impact in Korea. On March 1, 1919, a Proclamation of Korean Independence was issued by 33 prominent Koreans. This is exactly similar to the Proclamation of Complete Independence on 26th January 1930 under the leadership of Mahatma Gandhi and Jawaharlal Nehru, throughout the whole of India. Similarly, in Korea, about 50,000 people took part in peaceful demonstrations wherever the proclamation was read. According to the Japanese reports during this movement for Independence in Korea which lasted in full vigour for two months, 533 Koreans were killed, 1409 wounded and 19,054 imprisoned. The Japanese Govt. being unpopular had to recall its Governor-General Yoshimichi Hasegawa and appointed Admiral Makoto Saito. However, many Korean patriots were agitating for Korean Independence outside Korea in Siberia, Manchuria, China and U.S.A. This was similarly done during Indian freedom struggle, when many Indian patriots tried to mobilize world opinion in favour of India's·Independence. It was Gandhi's great ingenuity that he could enlist the active support of many eminent Britishers, prominent Europeans and Americans in his "battle of right against might." Again, an exactly exciting similar dimension we can find in the Freedom Movements both in Korea and India, to install National Governments in exile. The Korean nationalists abroad after the March Movement, set up a provisional government with Headquarters in Sanghai. This is similar to setting up Free India Govt. in exide by Raja Mahendra Pratap and later by Subhas Chandra Bose in South Asia in 1946. Mr. Bose not only set up a full-fledged parallel Govt. but also set up Indian National Army which fought the Britishers in Burma and also inside India boarder. The Korean nationalists also continued their activities outside their country up to War II. A permanent Korean Commission was established in Washington D.C. They were also active even in Japan and an unsuccessful attempt was made on the life of Japanese Emperor to avenge the cruel repression by the Japanese rulers. In India one Indian youth avenged the brutal mass massacre of peaceful Indians at Jallianwala bagh by killing the king pin of this sordid inhuman drama of mass-murder. However, World War II brought an end to both Japanese rule in Korea and British rule in India. A provisional government in Korea was set up in 1946, so it was in India. Due to reasons beyond their control, both Korea and India suffered the torments of partition. There was war between the South and North Korea which lasted for three years in which one million lives were lost. India also in the wake of partition, an undeclared civil war in the form of communal riots ravaged both Pakistan and India resulting in not only the death of almost one hundred thousands people but displacement of more than 30 million people and that has followed three broader wars. But I am constrained to believe that these wars are the result of colonial legacy which works on Divide and Rule Policy.

II

Apart form similarity in the strategies of Freedom Movement between Korea and India, there is deeper cultural and spiritual roots between them. If legends are to be believed, India and Korea enjoy a pre-historic relationship. During the 1st century A.D., a Korean king named Kim-Suro of Kaya kingdom had married a Princess of *Ayodhya*, the kingdom of the great Indian hero and incarnation Lord Ram. During the Mahabharata period, the dynasty of the *Kurus* are said to have gone upto Korea in pursuit of cultural Odyssey. Coming to the more recent and the period of recorded history, Buddhism has been a strong bond between Korea and India. Buddhism is perhaps the most precious gift that the far eastern countries received from India, which is the homeland of Buddhism. However, as Korea being surrounded on three sides by the sea, Buddhism found its way to Korea as a result of the influence of China. Buddhism came to Korea as early as in the 4th century A.D. and slowly through the benevolent royal patronage of kingdoms of *Shilla*, *Koquryo* (328 A.D.), *Paekche* (600 A.D.), *Karyo* (918-1392 A.D.), and through the scholarly dedication of some for the Indian monks like Sundo (4th century A.D.), Maranand (384 A.D.), *Kukhejha* (4th Century A.D.) and Korean Bhikkhus like *Kutik* (who studied in India) that

Buddhism began to be practised by the common people and it became the life-pattern of India. Even killing of animals was regarded as a wrong act. However, due to many reasons, there was decline of Buddhism. The *YI* dynasty (1392-1910 A.D.) adopted Confucianism in 1910. With the Japanese occupation of Korea, there was an attempt to introduce into Korea Buddhist sects affiliated to Japan. But anti-Japanese mood of the Koreans did not welcome it. Today one third of population in Korea are Buddhists. There are 7244 Buddhist temples, 22200 Bhikkhus and even some full-fledged Buddhist Universities.

Although the golden days of Buddhism both in Korea and India have become mostly the glories of the past, we cannot deny that there is still strong impact of Buddhistic ideals on life-pattern including the Freedom Movement of both countries. Gandhi has inherited the Buddhist legacy of compassion and non-violence, which signifies a state of complete peace and harmony in the life of the individual as well as the society as a whole. In the Buddhist tradition, the penacle is reached in the spiritual state of *Brahma-Vihara,* which implies the inculcation, nourishing and development of the four-fold sublime States-friendliness (*mettā*), compassion (*Karunā*), loving kindness (*muditā*) and equanimity (*Upekhā*)[3]. Of the five precepts (*Panch-Shila*), of Buddhism, "abstination from taking life" of others is the first one. The very idea of "the well-being of all" (*Sabbe Satta Bhavantu Sukhitatta*)[4] also positively suggests the idea of non-violence (*Ahimsā*). Hence, non-violence is the most important concept of Buddhist tradition. But it does not mean a weapon of the weak and surrender to injustice. Buddha fearlessly carried the war into the enemy's camp and brought down on its knees an arrogant priesthood. But even as Buddha indulged in intense direct action, he showed unmistakable love and gentleness behind his action. Hence, he is no follower of Buddha, who being afraid to die, takes flight before any danger, all the while wishing that somebody else would remove the danger by destroying the person causing it.

To Gandhi, "non-violence is a universal principle and its operation is not limited by a hostile environment. Indeed, its efficacy can be tested only when it acts in the midst of and in spite of opposition".[4A] (CH. 30.6.38). Our non-violence would be hollow thing and nothing worth, if it depended for its success on the goodwill of the authorities. Like a practical idealist, to Gandhi, "truth and non-violence are no cloistered virtues but applicable as much in the forum and the legislatures as in the market place.[4B] (H. 8.5.37). So Gandhi did not agree with those that truth and non-violence base no place in politics or freedom struggle. He had no use for truth and non-violence as a means of individual salvation. Their application in everyday life had been his life-long-experiment. *Secondly,* he did not like truth and non-violence to remain for more individual practice but for practice by groups and communities and nations. Non-violence is the attribute of the soul, and therefore, to be practised by everybody in all affairs of life.

Freedom is everybody's birth right. But "it can never be a free gift by one nation to another. It is a treasure to be purchases with a nation's best blood".[5] There is no such thing as slow freedom. Freedom is like a birth. Till we are fully free, we are slaves. All birth takes place in a moment.[6] Gandhi knew the price of freedom. He said: "In our march towards true freedom, we must be prepared for repitions of the wrong such as Jallianwala Bagh massacre.[7] He was convinced that "no country has ever risen without being purified through the force of suffering. The mother suffers so that her child may live. The condition of wheat growing is that the seed grain should perish".[8] He further exhorts: "That nation is great which rests its head upon death as its pillow".[9] "A nation that is capable of limitless sacrifice is capable of rising to limitless heights".[10]

But in his fearlessness, he did not see the exchange of British brute force for any other brute force. He contended that the revolutionary method of violence cannot succeed in India. He wrote his master-key book *Hind Swaraj* or *Indian Home Rule* (1908) in answer to the Indian school of violence. He had come into contact with every known anarchist in London. Their bravery impressed him but he felt that their zeal was misguided. But he felt that violence was no remedy for India's ills, and that her civilization required the use of a different higher weapon for self-protection. "The world is weary of hate. We see the fatigue overcoming the Western nations. We see that this song of hate has not benefited humanity. Let it be the privilege of India to turn a new leaf and act a lesson to the world".[11] One might of course say that there can be no non-violent rebellion and there has been none known to history. It was Gandhi's ambition to provide an instance, and it was his dream that his country may win its freedom through non-violence. He would like to repeat to the world times without number, and he with not purchase my country's freedom at the cost of non-violence. Gandhi had many reasons of discard violence as method of achieving freedom. "Science of war leads one to dictatorship pure and simple. Science of non-violence alone can lead one to pure democracy".[12] However, for argument sake, if we presume that India produced sufficient arms and ammunition and men who knew the art of war, it can be replied that in a non-violent war even women and children would contribute an equal share with physically the strongest. His resistance to war does not carry him to the point of thwarting those who wish to take part in it but Gandhi reasoned with them.

He put before them the better way and leave them to make the choice. According to him it is beneath the dignity of men to resort to mutual slaughter. He could afford to look at the butchery going on in the world with indifference. People might well applaud whole-heartedly the action of Mustafa Kamal Pasha, De Valera and Lenin. But India was not like Turkey or Ireland or Russia. His accumulated experience of more than fifty years in South Africa and India filled him with the greatest hope that in the adoption of non-violence lies the future of India and the world. Infact, Gandhi had to choose between allying himself to violence or finding out some other method of meeting the crisis". "Thus came into being the moral equivalent of war".[13] He distinguished between evil and evil-doer. He must not barbour ill-will or bitterness against the latter. Hence, his motto of life was to try to overcome evil by good, anger by love, untruth by truth, *himsa* by *ahimsa*.[14] Gandhi held himself to be incapable of hating any being on earth. Hate is the subtlest form of violence. We cannot be really non-violent and yet have hate in us".[15] It seems that Gandhi is Buddha born again. Lord Buddha says: "From anger, anger is not saliated". There is no fire like passion (*Rāga*), no losing through like hatred, there is no pain like this body, there is not happiness higher than rest".[16] We should also remember that the modern state has become more powerful that Liviathan, because of progress in science and technology. Hence, it is more difficult to fact the modern state with sporadic violence or terrorism. Besides, violence leads to counter-violence which never ends. Often it leads to civil war as we find in Bosnia, Afganistan, Burma, Kampuchea etc. Even recent history is a witness that a violent revolution in France has led to the emergence of a dictator like Napolean, in England, murder of Charles I, brought Cromwell and in Russia the Czar was replaced by Stalin. It means that a violent struggle endangers democratic fibre besides creating a climate of suspicion, hatred, revenge and violence, as they are the result of hopes long-deferred and aspirations ruthlessly suppressed.[17] In violent struggle even the legitimate participation is not possible. If we depend upon the barrel of the gun for the vindication of our cause, then one who can yield greater violence may claim that justice lies in his side. A revolution cannot be identified with violence otherwise even acts of murder of every bloody war however unjust they might be will be called revolution. "Violence may destroy one or more bad rulers, but like Ravana's head, others will pop up in their places".[18]

Gandhi's mission was more than achieving India's Independence. He endeavoured to show to his countrymen that "violent non-cooperation only multiplies evil"[19] and "the religion of non-violence is not meant merely for the *rishis* and saints. It is meant for common people as well. Non-violence is the law of our species as violence is the law of the brute... The dignity of man requires obedience to a higher law—to the strength of the spirit... The *rishis* (seers), who discovered the law of non-violence in the midst of violence, were greater geneouses than Newton. They were themselves greater warrior than Wellington. Having themselves known the use of arms, they realized their uselessness and taught a weary world that its salvation lay not through violence but through non-violence".[20] It was Gandhi's ambition and dream that his country win its freedom through non-violence. And as he said he "would like to repeat to the world times without number that I will not purchase my country's freedom at the cost of non-violence." My marriage to non-violence is such an absolute thing that I would rather commit suicide than he deflected from my position.[21] True democracy can never come through untruthful and violent means. Individual freedom can have the fullest play only under a regime of unadulterated *ahimsa*.[22] In its positive form, non-violence means the largest love, the greatest charity. "Having flung aside the sword, there is nothing except the cup of love which I can offer to those who oppose me"[23] —he said. He could not think of a permanent amenity between man and man. Love is the strongest force the world possesses." The hardest heart and the grossest ignorance must disappear before the rising sun of suffering without anger and without malice".[24] His goal was friendship with the whole world and "he could combine the greatest love with the greatest opposition to wrong".[25] However, Gandhi's non-violence was "not merely a passive spirituality that spends itself in idle meditation, but it will be an active thing which will carry war into the enemy's camp.[26] Non-violence presupposes ability to strike. It has no room either for cowardice or vegenence. There is hope for a violent man to be same day non-violent but there is none for a coward. Non-violence and cowardice go ill together. Similarly vegenence too is a weakness, which comes out of tear of harm. But non-violence is impossible without fearlessness. Hence he said: "where there is choice between cowardice and violence, I would advice violence".[27] "I would risk violence a thousand times than the emasculation of a whole race".[28] But there are limitations of violence. It is intended to exert pressure, but it is the insane pressure of anger and ill-will, while non-violent act exert pressure for more effective than violent act, for that pressure comes from goodwill and gentleness. It works subtly and invisibly, it is the surest and quickest way.

Conclusion

It is believed that there can be no non-violent rebellion and there has been none known to history. Koreans and Indian freedom struggle of the recent past have atleast partially refuted this belief. Perhaps, both Korea and India have the common legacy of spirituality and compassion of Buddha. Apart from Lord Buddha, India has a continuing tradition of non-violence from the ancient Vedas upto Gandhi. Non-violence is regarded as the supreme virtue. However, it was, Gandhi who brought non-violence from the high pedestal of individual virtue to the religion of the common men. It is a universal principle applicable as much in the forum and the legislatures as in the market place. It has place in politics and worldly affairs. Then, it is not matters for mere individual practice but for social action also. Gandhi has demonstrated the efficacy of non-violent massive mass-action during Indian Freedom Struggle. He adopted the double dynamics of agitational method (*Satyagraha*), (Strike, Demonstration, Boycott, Non-cooperation, Civil Disobedience, Fasting including Fast Unto Death) and *Constructive Programme* (like communal Harmony, Eradication of Indian Aparthied, Prohibition, Rural Industries, Basic Education, National Language, Service to Women, Tribal People, etc.). Constructive Programme is the construction of complete Independence. Non-violent direct action is an aid to constructive programme and is a full substitute for armed revolt. In fact, the goal of Constructive Programme is the achievement of Independence and it is achieved in the measure constructive programme is fulfilled.

Non-violent resistance is as old as resistance through violence. There has been examples of Socrates, Jesus and others. Gandhi tried to practice it on collective level. So we find in Korea in 1910 after Japanese occupation. But there are a few more instances of non-violent mass resistance During mid 19th Century (1860-67), when Emperor Franz Joseef's attempted to subjugate Hungry to the Austrian power and moderates felt helpless, a Catholic landowner Ferene Deak not only protested but also organised independent Hungarian education, agriculture and industry, and boycott of Jails, Parliament. There was also non-violent resistance against military action and finally Emperor had to give Hungry her constitution. The struggle against social and racial discrimination in South Africa was started in 1906 and there were appreciable achievements. In India, apart from National Struggle for Independence in 1921-22 (Non-cooperation), Civil Disobedience (1929-30), Individual Satyagraha (1940) and Quit India Movement (1942), there were successful non-violent mass action in Champaran (1917), Vykom (1925), Kotagarh (1921), Bardoli (1928), Ahmedabad (1917), Kheda (1926-27), Borsad (1923), Nagpur (1927), Salt Satyagraha (1930) were organised. *In Denmark,* in 1940 without previous preparation, training is non-violent resistance, Danish people organised defiance against ruthless Nazis. In Norway again in 1940, Non-violent Resistance was organised in which youth in atheletic clubs, judges of Supreme Court etc. participated. Education on Nazi pattern was boycotted. We know about non-violent resistance against seggregation laws in U.S.A. in 1955 under the leadership of Martin Luther King. In modern Poland, the Polish People started a non-violent mass action under Walesa against the Communist martial regime and they succeeded. Even in 1st World War coal miners of the Rhur in Germany non-violent resistance was organised. In Gold Coast, after 10 years of non-violent resistance, Nkrumah was freed. Recently, in U.S.S.R., it was non-violent mass action that had compelled the military leaders to free Gorachov. Even in Japan, under Rev. Fuji Guruji, a successful non-violent action was organized to stop Tokyo airport for nuclear base. In India during 1975-76, when civil rights were tranpled, a massive non-violent mass movement arose in which the then ruler and her party was thrown into the dustbin of history.

Violence has lost its dynamics. If we want a world

without war, we also should have a struggle for national independence without violence, terrorism. If we allow terrorism and violence, we cannot hope to banish nuclear war. Hence, either we have non-violent resistance or non-existence of the entire humanity.

REFERENCES

1. Poem by R.N. Tagore, Bengali translation by Deepak Ray 'Prachyer Deep'.

2. *Encyclopaedia Britannica*.

3. Gosh, I.M., *Ahimsa-Buddhism and Gandhian,* Delhi: Indian Bibliographies Bureau, 1988, Preface, V.

4. *Ibid.,* p. 59. See *Dhammapada,* Verse 270 (ed. S. Radhakrishnan, Oxford University Press, 1950).

4A. Gandhi, M.K., *Harijan,* 30.6.38.

4B. *Ibid.,* 8.5.37.

5. Gandhi, M.K., *Young India,* 5.1.1922.

6. *Ibid.,* 9.3.1922.

7. *Ibid.,* 18.2.1920.

8. *Ibid.,* 16.6.1920.

9. Gandhi, M.K., *Hind Swaraj* or *Indian Home Rule,* Ahmedabad, Navajivan Publishing House, 1944, p. 48.

10. Gandhi, M.K., *Young India,* 25.8.1920.

11. Gandhi, M.K., Gandhi in Indian Village, by M. Desai, Madras : S. Ganesan, 1927, p. 166.

12. Gandhi, M.K., *Harijan,* 3.10.1938.

13. *Ibid., Young India,* 5.11.1931.

14. *Ibid.,* 8.8.1929.

15. *Ibid.,* 17.8.1934.

16. *Dhammapada*, 251 (Mala Vaggo).
17. Young, K., *Social Psychology*, London : Kegan Paul, p. 439.
18. Gandhi, M.K., *Harijan*, 21.9.1934.
19. *Ibid., Young India*, 23.3.1922.
20. *Ibid.*, 11.8.1920.
21. *Ibid.*, 12.11.1932.
22. Gandhi, M.K., *Harijan*, 27.5.1939.
23. *Ibid., Young India*, 2.4.1931.
24. *Ibid.*, 29.2.1925.
25. *Ibid.*, 10.3.1920.
26. *Ibid.*, 12.5.1920.
27. *Ibid.*, 11.8.1920.
28. *Ibid., Harijan*, 20.7.1935.

Chapter 8

CONSTRUCTIVE PROGRAMME AS CONSTRUCTIVE REVOLUTION : A GANDHIAN APPRAISAL

Ideological Perspective

"Hitherto the word 'revolution' has been connected with *violence* and has as such been conceived by established authority".[1] However, Gandhian revolution is not a 'revolt', it is an evolutionary revolution, it is a 'bloodless revolution'. Hence, it is "a revolution of thought, of spirit. It is a process of purification and as such, it constitutes a revolution in one's ideas".[2] The essence of revolution is, no doubt, change; of course, it is a kind of change which is distinguished by its scope and speed. The term 'revolution', outside the natural science, connotes a '*sweeping*' and '*sudden*' change in the entire power structure of the whole society. It is a major break in continuity of development in the old and existing order. Hence, the essence of revolution is "*sudden* and *thorough-going* change", not the violent upheaval which frequently accompanies it. On the other hand, genuine revolution is a social phenomenon that starts well in advance of the violent manifestation. Violence is, therefore, the overt evidence that the change has occurred. For example, the ground-work for the great revolutions like the English, the American, the French, even the Bolshivics and the Chinese were prepared much ahead in the minds of the people as a cultural crisis. Revolutions are work of the *principles* than of bayonets. If we identify revolution with violence, they every act of murder, bloody war however unjust they might be called revolutions. But we know that a real revolution always means a "fundamental change in our ideas and ideology, ethos and values of life". And it is foolish to believe that we can change one's ideas or ideologies through some external physical force". "Coercion can create some pattern of uniformity but it cannot change heart and mind of man".[3] To say that if we can change the societal structure, the individuals will be changed is only a half-truth, for man is not a Pavlovian dog fit to be conditioned and reconditioned in accordance to scheme of some self-made master having some political power. Besides, it is human nature to react to force. Hence, the more of violence, the less of revolution. Bloodshed creates *upheavals* but not revolutions.[4] Confiscation of property may be called a *rebellion* but again not a revolution.[5] Those who think that our attitudes and opinions can never change betray an aweful ignorance of human psychology and enormous mobility of man and plasticity of human nature. True, society influences man but man also creates history. In fact, the dynamics of change involves the idea of triple-transformation-of *heart*, (*hridy-Parivartana*), *head* (*vichara-parivartana*), and *social situation* (*sthiti-parivartana*). The theory of material basis of revolution is therefore one-sided. Social and political changes in history have been caused more by changed ideas and values than by material causes. Hence, Gandhi had to choose between allying himself to evidence or finding out another civilized but effective method of social change. Civilization requires use of a different higher weapon of fighting injustice. This is also based on the recognition of superiority of the *soul-force* over the *brute-force*. "The sum total of energy of mankind is not to bring us down but to lift us up, and that is the result of the definite, if unconscious, working of the law of love.[7] Gandhi believes that the "human society is a ceaseless growth, an unfoldment in terms of spirituality".[8]

This led Gandhi to invent "moral equivalent of war" or *Satyagraha*, which tries to replace body-force (*sharirbal*), gun-force (*topbal*), and force of arms (*hatyarbal*) by the soul-force and force of suffering. Satyagraha had two dimensions—*(a) Agitational* including various methods of direct non-violent action like strikes, boycott, non-cooperation, civil-disobedience, fasting etc. and *(b) Constructive Programmes*, which are indirect methods of non-violent social action like communal harmony, eradication of untouchability, Khadi and village industries, prohibition, village sanitation, New Education etc. He tried to incorporate some of these constructive programmes into the agenda of the freedom movement. However, many of the great leaders became not only sceptical but also regarded it an escapist venture, if not a retrograde strategy. What they needed was a fighting and militant programme of action, which is the legacy of ideology of political violence. Gandhi's *Hind Swaraj* (1908) was also written in an "answer to the Indian school of violence". He was convinced that violence was not remedy for India's ills, and that her civilization required the use of a different and higher weapon for self-protection.[9] In order to dispel the misconceptions about the role of constructive programme in freedom movement, Gandhi wrote a small booklet *Constructive Programme*[10] in 1941 which was revised and enlarged in 1945 enumerating 18 itmes.

According to Gandhi, "the Constructive Programme may otherwise and more fittingly be called Construction of Poorna Swaraj or complete Independence by truthful and non-violent means.[11] He was so much convinced of its efficacy that according to him, "if it could be successfully worked out, the end of it would be Independence we want. But it requires the result of the entire people to take up. the various construction programmes. However, it has never happened in totality. Hence the attainment of freedom took up longer time. Hence, they are also relevant today to make out Independence more meaningful and complete. There is still no substitute for it to usher non-violent socio-economic change in society. Practice, no doubt, will always fall short of the theory, even as the drawn line falls short of the theoretical line of Euclid. Therefore, complete independence will be complete only to the extent of our approach in practice to truth and non-violence. On the other hand, there is no such thing as an imaginary or even perfect definition of Indepedence through violence, which presupposes only ascendancy of a person or a party of the nation which makes the most effective use of violence. Hence, perfect equality, economic or otherwise is inconceivable in a violent revolution.

The aims of both *i.e., Satyagraha* and *Constructive Programme* are the same and there is no conflict between the two. Constructive Programme serve both as condition and prepatory ground for ushering Civil Disobedience. They also serve to consolidate the gains of Civil Disobedience. Even Dr. R.M. Lohia, the stormy petrol of non-violent direct action, advanced three symbols of social change—*Jail* (Civil Disobedience), *Fawrā* (Weapons for manual work) and *Vote* (Political awareness). It is said that even Comrade Lenin, after the victory of Bolshivika revolution, introduced voluntary manual work one day in a week. When some body questioned its rationale after the establishment of the Socialist State, Lenin politely said: "This is the beginning of socialism".

Constructive Programme has three functions—(1)

Redressal of a local wrongs; (2) To rouse local consciousness and conscience; (3) Individual Satyagraha. Hence, it has almost all elements of a Satyagraha.[12] Without cooperation of the millions by way of Constructive Programme, Civil Disobedience would have been a mere bravado and worse than useless. To think that Constructive Programme is not a militant or dynamic programme, like Non-Cooperation and Civil Disobedience is an utter misconception. We falsely think that only strikes, *bandhs* and *qheraos* can prepare the masses for a social action or self-rule. On the contrary, "the true building up of Swaraj consists in the millions of the India wholeheartedly working for the Constructive Programme. Without first engaging themselves in the Constructive Programme, the "whole nation cannot rise from its age-long torpor, whether the British remain or not, it is our duty always to wipe out unemployment, to bridge the gulf between rich and poor, to banish communal strife, to exercise the demon of untouchability... If the crores of people take a living interest in this nation- building work, freedom must not remain a dream and unattainable by either non-violence or violence".[13] Civil Disobedience is but a minor part of Satyagraha.[14] Civil Disobedience is not absolutely necessary to win freedom through purely non-violent efforts, if the cooperation is secured in the Constructive Programme.[15] Such is the importance of Constructive Programme in the eyes of Mahatma Gandhi. Let us deleinate some of its obvious characteristics :

(*a*) Constructive Programme as a Nation Building Action

Even after fifty years of independence, we have been griviously striving to preserve our unity and integrity. Even, today, Muslim separatism has been matched by Sikh and neo-Hindu fundamentalism. Communal problems are still regarded as the most sensitive issue of the nation.

In a multi-religious, multi-ethnic society like ours, communal and social tensions are bound to occur and reoccur. Gandhi had provision of this problem. Hence, Communal Unity was priority no one in the list of his Constructive Programme. However, he knew that unity does not mean political unity which may be imposed. It means an unbreakable heart unity....[16] In order to realize this, he desired that every Congressman to cultivate personal friendship with persons representing other faiths other than his own. He should have the same regard for the other faiths so he has for his own. "Living unity can never come out of artificial entities being brought together on a common platform.[17] If we could have heeded to Gandhi's advice, there would have been no partition. But neither the Muslims nor the Hindus listened to him and they behaved like and wolves and tigers. So in the case of partition of India, Gandhi did not fail but we have failed him in Calcutta, Noakhali, Bihar, Punjab and Delhi. As a result, the Muslim League got a bloody Pakistan and the Hindu fundamentalists got satisfied with Gandhi's blood and legacy of communal politics. The cancer of communalism is still seen in occasional communal riots between Hindus and Muslims and Hindus and Sikhs. Hence communal harmony is more relevant today than before.

Like communal harmony, removal of untouchability had become his life-mission. He had advised every Hindu to make common cause with them and be friend them in their awful isolation[18] —which the world has never seen. He never looked upon the programme as a mere legislative or political play but something indespensable for building the edifice of Swaraj. He tried to touch their heart. He named the untouchables as Harijan, he lived among them in Bhangi colony, he would bless a married couple only when one of the partners was a Harijan; he collected funds for Harijan uplift; he led their entry into temple inspite of opposition from orthodox Hindus. Once he was hit by a *lathi* blow on his head and a bomb was thrown in his meeting for supporting the cause of the Untouchables. Through his inspiration, hundred of upper caste Hindus dedicated themselves to the cause of removal of this immoral Indian aparthied. It is mostly due to his Harijan uplift movement that granting reservation in government jobs through constitutional provisions was no problem. This is an example of achieving social justice without confrontation. All these are unique attempts of nation-building by breaking alienation one fourth of Hindu population from the main body. Similarly, he included service of *adivasis* as a part of his constructive programme. All such service is not merely humanitarian but solidly national, and brings us nearer to true independence.[19] Regarding women, Gandhi felt that "women have been taught to regard themselves as slaves of men. Men have not realized this truth in its fulness in their behaviour towards women.[20] He wanted to see that they enable them to realize their full status and play their part as equals.[21] Gandhi through his Freedom Movement brought India's women out from their darkness as nothing else could have in such incredibly short space of time.[22] Thus Gandhi helped in nation-building. He was not building nation only on social level but above on cultural and educational levels. It is a tragedy that even after 50 years of Independence, about half of the illiterate population of the whole world are placed in India. Besides, the education that is imparted has neither the capacity to provide livelihood nor life of character. He set up the Hindustani Talimi Sangh to transform village children into model villagers. Primary education is a force designed without regard to the want of India. Basic education, therefore, links the children to all that is best and lasting. It develops both the body and the mind, and keeps the child rooted to the soil with a glorious vision of the future.[23] Together with regular scheme of Basic Education, he advocated functional adult education. He was not satisfied with mere literacy as it soon relapses into illiteracy. Through adult education, he wanted to give political and civic education, lessons in public hygiene, and some knowledge of crafts. Today, our formal education in schools and colleges is a clossal failure because education they receive is merely literary and it makes them unfit for manual work in after-life. The pupils forget dignity of labour and have turned into white collared elites. Education has become a vested interest as the fees in so-called 'public schools' are beyond the reach of the common public. The nation is not in a position to provide school building, and teachers for all our children. However, if we introduce some craft or learning by doing, education will be meaningful and can contribute somethings to meet the cost of education. Today, the Universities have become workshops to create unemployed persons. Besides, they are unfamiliar either with their surroundings or values of life. There has been total destruction of Indian ethos. The child feels no poetry about the home life. The village are all a sealed book to him. His own civilization is presented to him as imbecile, barbarous and useless for all practical purposes.[24] Hence Gandhi's Nai Talim with its emphasis on all round development of hand, heart and heard and social and national progress was the solid foundation of a strong nation.

(b) Constructive Programme as a Programme of Social Transformation

If we look to the various items of Constructive Programme like the development of Khadi and Village Industries, emphasis upon economic equality, organisation and uplift of Kisans, Labour, Students, encouragement to Provincial and National Languages, we find a concrete blue print of social transformation. For example his emphasis upon Khadi and Village Industries was a silent and slow method of provide employment to lakhs of under-employed people leaving in villages who live on agriculture that hardly gives jobs for six months a year. It was not sailing against a headwind nor taking the country to the dark ages. In a country with such a vast population and small capital what we need is small scale labour-intensive indigenous industires. The so-called new economic reforms have created more unemployment, have drained more national resources to foreign countries encouraged corruption and criminalisation of politics. The economic inequality has risen very far. However to Gandhi economic equality is the master-key to non-violent Independence. According to him, "a violent and bloody revolution is a certainty one day unless there is a voluntary abdication of riches and the power that riches give and sharing them for the common good".[25] He had advocated 'trusteeship' so that to eliminate the curse of private ownership and strife between capital and labour. Apart from economic transformation, he was also concerned with moral and cultural transformation like the curse of intoxicants and narcotics. He waged a crusade against drinks and drugs. Today, it can save atleasts 35000 crores of rupees that go out of consumer's pocket besides bestowing upon them many diseases and mental and moral degradation.

(c) Constructive Programme as a Programme of Mass-Contact and Public Training

Constructive Programme is for non-violent army what drilling etc. is for an army designed for bloody warfare. No progress of Satyagraha is possible without Constructive Programme as it creates a sense of self-purification and selfless service. "It is a collective training for social change".[26] For social change, we need mass-contact. "There is non non-violent disobedience without sustained constructive effort. A living continous mass contact is impossible without some Constructive Programme reducing almost daily contact of workers with the masses".[27] They are most effective method of mass-contact. The selfless service touches the heart and generates trust. Here it is not only a cheap propaganda but a direct social service. In fact, Individual Constructive Programme among an unprepared people and by leaders not known to or trusted by them is of no avail, and mass civil disobedience is an impossibility.

(d) Constructive Programme as Instrument of Social Awareness

Through mass-contact, "an idea of exploitation-free social and economic order" is also inculcated in the people. Thus the Constructive Programme" are like weapons of war.[28] When awareness is tried to be created only through public speeches, it is not so effective. But when some Constructive Programmes are carried out, people get object lessons in their merits, as those programmes are action-oriented. People witness concrete results. For example, when prohibition programme is launched, people see that it is a vital social reform. When some die-hard drunkards and opium addicts are weared from this curse, people witness a moral regeneration. A strong awareness is generated. Hence, Gandhi made Constructive Programme as an integral part of the national freedom movement and therefore of the Civil Disobedience. "Civil Disobedience without the backing of the constructive programme is criminal and a waste of effort".[29] All cannot court imprisonment but can work for Constructive Programme. Even in armed conflict army is powerfully helped by civil population. People engaged in Constructive Programme try to preserve communal unity, lessen the antagonism from the Harijans, etc. and boost up the morale of the people, while the Civil Disobedience goes into full swing. Satyagraha as a weapon in the struggle for freedom, exhausts its potentialities and also looks to the dynamic situation, pregnant with immense potentialities of mass revolutionary outbreaks, simply because it is not supported by Constructive Programme.

(*e*) Constructive Programme as Instrument of Self-reliance

Constructive Programme, through its programmes of Khadi and Village Industries, tries to encourage "economic freedom and equality of all in the country".[30] It means a wholesale swadeshi mentality, a determination to find all the necessaries of life in India and that too through the labour and intellect of the villagers".[31] Khadi mentality means decentralization of the production and distribution of the necessaries of life". Therefore the formula evolved is, very village is to produce all its necessaries and a certain percentage in addition for the requirements of the cities. Village industries come in as a handmaid to *Khadi.* They cannot exist without *Khadi* and *Khadi* will be robbed of its dignity without them. Village economy cannot be complete without the essential village industries such as hand-grinding, hand-pounding, oil-pressing etc. All should make it a point of honour to use only village articles whenever and wherever available. "Given the demand there is no doubt that most of our wants can be supplied from our villages. When we have become village-minded, we will not want imitations of the west or machine-made products, but we will develop a true national taste".[32] Since the wanton destruction of village industries, intelligence and brightness have fled from the villages, leaving them inane, lustreless, and reduced almost to the state of their illkept cattle. If this spirit of Swadeshi can be revived today, we can face the onslaught of multi-national companies and their exploitation.

(*f*) Constructive Programme as basis of a Socialist Society

The soul of Constructive Programme lies in voluntarism. Swaraj means a continuous attempt to free ourselves from the government regulations. It does not mean whether the government is an alien government or our own. If after the coming of Swaraj, the people of India will keep on looking to the government for regulating every detail of their lives, then that Swaraj will be meaningless." So his conception of Swaraj was "Home Rule". He "looked upon an increase in the power of the State with the greatest fear, because although while apparently doing good by minimizing exploitation, it does the greatest harm to mankind by destroying individuality which lies at the root of all progress".[33] His Constructive Programme was an Indian alternative to establishment of an equalitarian socialist society, where there would be the least interference of the State. He had, therefore, floated voluntary institutions in every field—Panchayat in political Self-Government, A.I. Spinners Association and Village Industries Association in economic field, and A.I. Harijan Sevak Sangh, A.I. Adivasi Kalyan Sangh, A.I. Prohibition Council etc. in social and cultural fields. After Gandhi's death, Sarvodaya Samaj and Sarva-Seva-Sangh have been created for carrying out those constructive work on voluntary basis. The entire Bhoodan-Gramdan movement was an extension of voluntarism on a massive scale. Even Jaya Prakash Narain had tried to encourage voluntarism by establishing Association of Voluntary Association (AVARD) and guiding A.I. Panchayat Parishad for flowering grass-root democracy at village level. National Alliance of peoples is spearheading its movement against ever-spreading tantacles of the multinationals. In short, Constructive Programme is an instrument of self-confidence and self-reliance.

(g) Constructive Programme as a Consensus Method of Social Change

Dr. Rajendra Prasad in his book on "Constructive Programme" has pointed out its unique feature that it is generally acceptable by all sections of society. There is much less scope for controversies and confrontations. Anyone can participate into its working. There is adequate expression for self expression. One who involves himself in any of its programme gets self-confidence and self-satisfaction, as its result is almost immediately visible. Hence it is not like any business in credit but throughly a business in cash. In agitational programmes like Non-cooperation and Civil Disobedience, one is liable to get punishment and loose his job or property. Everybody cannot bear the strain of agitational programme. But in most of the Constructive Programmes, so much difficulties arise. It is more a revolution in person. In this way, it is more a revolution in person. In this way, it is more foundational and solid base of social change, done silently. There are many humanitarian work also like service to the leper, village sanitation etc. that generates public sympathy. A bond of trust is created between the worker and the people so that even a full fledged agitation is launched, support from average citizens becomes spontaneous.

(h) Constructive Programme as a Model of Practical Idealism

There is essential connection between Constructive Programme and Civil Disobedience. Constructive Programme is not essential for local civil disobedience for specific relief as in the case of Bardoli. Tangible common grievance restricted to a particular locality is enough. But for such an indefinable thing as Swaraj, people must have previous training,[34] for which Constructive Programme is like drilling of the army. Individual Civil Disobedience among an unprepared people and by leaders not known to or trusted by them is of no avail, and mass civil disobedience is an impossibility. The more therefore the progress of the Constructive Programme, the greater is there the chance for the success of civil Disobedience. Secondly, there are limitation to agitational methods. We also need staying power in a long drawn struggle and so it preserves morale. One cannot afford to go on for agitation *ad infinitum* as the soldiers are not supposed to be on the front for too long a period. But this does not take away the thrill and romance of Constructive Programme. If there can be thrill in breaking a bottle of liquor, it is perhaps more exciting to see a person taking a vow to abstain from drink for the entire life or making an illiterate able to read and write or so on.

Conclusion

Constructive Programme may be looked differently if they are placed in different positions. For example, "the *Charkha* in the hands of a poor widow brings a paltry pice to her, in the hands of Jawaharlal it is an instrument of India's freedom. It is the office assigned to constructive programme which gives it an irresistible prestige and power".[35] He was therefore convinced that "handling of Civil Disobedience without the Constructive Programme will be like an paralyzed hand attempting to lift a spoon".[36] Gandhi did not conceive his mission to be that of a knight-errant wandering everywhere to deliver people from difficult situations. His humble occupation had been to show people how they can solve their own difficulties. Thus Constructive Programme is a programme of self-help. It is not necessary that we should organise one such constructive programme on a national or international level. As a rule, small groups work better than larger groups for there are strong personal bonds between them. Everyone participates in the common task and gets the joy of its achievement. The most remarkable thing about constructive programme is that it ushers a silent revolution without propaganda or noise. The work it does is its best publicity. Unlike agitational programme, constructive programme performs the work of social change in its working. There is no lactation period. As forced sacrifice is no sacrifice, so emotional resolve do not last. These days, we are fed up with such agitational programmes like strikes, lockouts, processions, gherao, *dharnas, bandhs,* etc. we need an alternative of protest. Recently, Kerala High Court has banned *bandhs* and that is confirmed by the Supreme Court of India. This shows that the dynamics of agitational methods have become work out. In this context, Gandian method of Constructive Programme is psychologically more suitable. It wins the sympathy of the adversaries and support of the people. But silently and steadily, it goes on changing the both the individual temperament as will as the basic socio-economic structure of society. Hence Constructive Programme is the key to Constructive Revolution.

REFERENCES

1. Gandhi, M.K. *Young India,* 30.3.1921.
2. *Ibid.*
3. Bhave, V., *Bhoodan* (English Weekly), Varanasi, June 9, 1956.
4. Bang, T.D., *Kranti Ki Pukar* (Hindi), Varanasi: A.B. Sarva Seva Sangh, 1956, pp. 36-37.
5. Dharmadhikari, D., *Kranti Ka Agla Kadam* (Hindi), Varanasi: A.B.S.S. 1955, p. 51, *Manviya-Kranti* (Hindi), Varanasi: A.B.S.S., 1955, p. 18.

6. Gandhi, M.K., *Hind Swaraj,* Ahmedabad, Navajivan Publishing House, 1st edition, 1938,Ch XVI.
7. *Ibid., Young India,* 12.11.1931.
8. *Ibid., Young India,* 16.9.26.
9. *Ibid., Hind Swaraj,* 'A word of Explanation', Jan. 1921, pp. 15.
10. *Ibid., Constructive Programme: Its Meaning and Place,* Ahmedabad, Navajivan Publishig House, 1941.
11. *Ibid.,* p. 7 (Introductory).
12. Gandhi, M.K. *Gandhi's Correspondence with the Government,* 1942-44, Ahmedabad : Navajivan Publishing House, 1945, p. 146.
13. *Ibid.,* p. 354.
14. Gandhi, M.K., *Harijan,* 25.3.1939.
15. Gandhi, M.K., Gandhi's Correspondence with the Govt., p. 354.
16. Gandhi, M.K., *Construcitve Programme,* p. 8.
17. *Ibid.,* p. 9.
18. *Ibid.,* p. 10.
19. *Ibid.,* p. 26.
20. *Ibid.,* p. 18.
21. *Ibid.,* p. 18.
22. *Ibid.,* p. 18.
23. *Ibid.,* p. 16.
24. Gandhi, M.K., *Young India,* 1.9.1921.
25. Gandhi, M.K., *Constructive Programme,* p. 22.
26. Gandhi, M.K., *Harijan,* 18.5.1940.

27. Gandhi, M.K., *Harijan*, 23.4.1940.
28. Gandhi, M.K., *Young India*, 23.1.1930.
29. Gandhi, M.K., *Congress Bulletin*, Allahabad, 8.1.42.
30. Gandhi, M.K., *Constructive Programme*, p. 12.
31. *Ibid.*, p. 11.
32. *Ibid.*, p. 15.
33. Gandhi, M.K., *Modern Review*, Calcutta, Oct. 1935, p. 412.
34. Gandhi, M.K., *Young India*, 9.3.1930.
35. Gandhi, M.K., *Constructive Programme*, p. 31.
36. *Ibid.*

Chapter 9

GLOBAL UNITY THROUGH SCIENCE AND TECHNOLOGY

In no other field Gandhi has been more misunderstood than in his attitude towards science and technology. Firstly, this is because of "in the urgency of his vision, he has used rather crude language" about machinery, which according to Prof. Burns "if he were revising the book, he would himself alter".[1] There are ample statements to prove that Gandhi has never attributed to mechanism "moral qualities". They belong to men, who use them, not in the mechanism. He said: "Machines will remain because, like the body, they are inevitable".[2] Gandhi has grown from truth to truth. His words and deeds were dictated by prevailing conditions. So we find changes in his views about science and technology.

In 1909, when he wrote *Hind Swaraj*, he was very very sore with machinery. To him, "it is machinery that has impoverished India..." "Machinery has began to desolate Europe. Ruination is now knocking at the English gate" it represents a great sin[3]... "Machinery is like a snake-hole which may contain from one to a hundred snakes".[4] He went to the extent : "I cannot recall a single good point in connection with machinery".[5] In 1919, he is on record to say, "There is thus room in the country for both the mill industry and the handloom weaving... I am not opposed to the movement of manufacturing machines in the country, nor in making improvement in the machinery... I am only concerned with what these machines are meant for,... whether these machines will be such as would blow off a million men in a minute or they will be such as would turn waste lands into arable and fertile land".[6] In 1922, he says : "I have nothing to say against the development of other industry in India by means of machinery, but I do say that to supply India with cloth manufactured either outside or inside, through gigantic mills is an economic blunder of the first magnitude. Just as it would be to supply cheap bread through bakeries established in the chief centres of India and to destroy the family stove".[7] In 1924, his famous statement is: "what I object to, is the craze for machinery, not machinery as such... Scientific truths and discoveries should first of all cease to be mere instruments of greed... The labourers will not be overworked and machinery instead of becoming a hindrance will be a help. I am aiming, not at eradication of all machinery, but limitations... The Supreme consideration is man".[8] In 1931, he explains the rationale : "I hold that the machinery method is harmful when the same thing can be done easily by millions of hands not otherwise occupied... If the craze for the machinery method continues, it is highly likely that a time will come when we shall be so incapacitated and weak that we shall begin to curse ourselves for having forgotten the use of the living machines given to us by God".[9] He further says that "Machinery is a grand and yet awful invention. If man controls the machines and allow them to control him, then they will entirely engulf civilization and everything".[10] In 1934, he opens another dimension of exploitation with machinery. Through spinning wheel, "we not only solve the question of unemployment but we declare that we have no intention of exploiting any nation, and we also end exploitation of the poor by the rich... We cannot industrialize ourselves, unless we make up our mind to enslave humanity".[11] In 1935, he **says** "machinery well used has to help and ease human effort. "The present use of machinery binds more and more to concentrate wealth in the hands of a few in total disregard of millions of men and women whose bread is snatched by it out of their months".[12] In 1936, responding to a Japanese correspondent who asked whether Gandhi was against the machine age, he said, "To say that is to carricature my views". I am not against machinery as such but I am totally opposed to it when it masters us... To another question—Would you not industrialize India ? Gandhi said: "I would indeed, in my sense of the term".[13] He meant rural industrialization which provides employment to many. In 1940, he said : "I have no interest in the machine nor (do) I oppose it. If I can produce my things myself, I became my master and so need no machinery".[14] In 1945, Gandhi opens another dimension *i.e.*, connection between machinery and violence. He says: Another danger in making more and more efforts for the protection of it, that is to say, we shall have to keep our army...".[15] In 1946, while addressing the Indian Industries Ministers' Conference said: "In a sense, man is the most wonderful machine in creation. It can be neither duplicated nor copied." He even welcomed the flush-system for improving the health of the city. I am opposed to machinery which displaces labour and leaves it idle.[16] In 1947, he is on record to admit: "Machine-power can make a valuable contribution towards economic progress. But a few capitalists have employed machine-power regardless of the interests of the common man that is why our condition has deteriorated today".[17]

Thus, we see an evolution in the attitude of Gandhi towards machine from 1909 to 1947.

We can briefly note down the salient features of Gandhi's multi-dimensional views about machinery and technology :

(1) Machinery is not the end but the means for human happiness. Man is the supreme consideration. Machine is for man, not man for machine.

(2) Gandhi challenged the technological basis of modern civilization and so he posited an alternative to the industrial technique of today.

(3) Any industrial technique must be geard to meet the basic human needs of food, clothing and housing.

(4) Gandhi was not against development of industry provided *(a)* it does not create unemployment, *(b)* it does not become an instrument of exploitation of man or nation, *(c)* it does not result in unlimited depradation of natural resources and resulting in pollution hazards, *(d)* it should not be used to concentrate wealth in the hands of a few in total disregard to millions, *(e)* it should foster decentralisation as centralisation cannot be sustained and defended without adequate force, *(f)* Instead of mass-production, he preferred production by masses and hence his insistence upon rural industrialisation, cottage and small industries, *(g)* Machinery should help and ease human effort so he welcomed the use of machinery which turns waste land into arable and fertile lands and removes the drudgery of man, *(h)* Production should be localised, *(i)* where heavy and large-scale industries are inevitable, they should be under producer's control.

Gandhi's ideas about machinery were the result of the ground realization of his own experience as well as that of his studies. When he read R.C. Dutt's Economic

History of India, he wept, his heart sickened. He had also read *Village Communities* by Maine, *Poverty and un-British Rule in India* by Dadabhai Naoroji, *The Fallacy of Speed* by Taylor, *Civilization : Its Cause and Cure* by Carpenter besides works of Tolstoy, Ruskin, Thoreau etc. Hence, it is neither his whim or idoyncracy but is inconsistent with his world-view.

Modern technology and industrialization has created manifold problems, not for one nation but for the whole world, and the entire humanity. Evils of unbridled industrialism has created crisis literature preoccupied with the theme of social disintegration and psycho-neurotic disorders 'resulting from the growth of an over-centralised, over mechanised industrial structure.[18] Man, however falliable and fallen, is much more than a machine.[19] Men have been entirely divorced from the world of nature.[20] This forced attinement of the human organism to the rigid and unnatural routines of the city, the factory and the machine has produced chronic, nerve-shattering tensions. There has been loss of permanent contact with natural elements, natural beings and rhythms has blunted and bifurcated sensibility.[21] Masses of men have been huddled into hideous over-crowded cities like cages of 'human spirit", which is a 'pathological phenomenon", the fountain source of divitalisation and delinquency. Modern technics with excessive specialisation have deprived of all spontaneity, creative, aesthetic joy and all personal and human significance. Researches show over 60% workers suffered badly from boredom in the metallurgical industry.[23] Mechanisation and automation have reduced man to mere clog in the wheel, where men are corrupted and degraded.[24] The report of *the Study of Conference on Human Problems of Industrial Communities*[25] came to the conclusion that industry was not end in itself UNESCO study complains of the lack of criminality satisfaction in modern culture.[26]

The *Price of progress* is too great for its results in a neurotic society. The crisis is clear. These who were impressed by success are now disillusioned by failure. It may be that 20th century will see our technological end by its own devices in a mighty shambles. Schumacher reechoes lamentation on the qualities of contemporary life. Mechanics and technics have became a source idolatory. This slavery dehumanizes man from within resulting in the loss of mediative, the creative and the spiritual enrichment.[27] True, technology has participated a revolution in mass-communication but the combination of the totalitarian monopoly of mass-media has also 'opened up opportunities of indoctrination without parallel in the past".[28] The refinement of technology have enabled the rulers to perfect and project their controls over the whole range of social life. Modern technology has made human labour more monstros. The lower classes have been emancipated, older ideals of a liberal society have been shattered. The Frankstein of modern technology has brought war nearer and created technological unemployment. We have seen the dangers of growing industrial hazards not only in the depletion of natural resources but also creating holes into the ozone layers. Hence machine qua machine is madness and source of decivilization of man, corruption and exploitation. Here we find a virtue surrender of human initiative, freedom and creativity. The Sabbath was made for man, not man for Sabbath. Should man live by proxy and machine do everything for him? The result will be endless irritability, discontent and revolt against work. Work is not the anti-thesis of life but a means of realising the full content of life. "No doubt we need leisure but a life of all leisure is a life of inferno for the soul of man".[29] Bernard Shaw, therefore, said, that perpetual holiday is the best definition of hell. Arnold Toynbee has demonstrated that *ease* and *luxury* has been the most fatal foes of 27 civilizations which have passed into oblivion of antiquity".[30] So is clear warning of John Galbraith against mad rush for industrialisation that we have become slaves of the machine.[31]

Hence Gandhi's critique of industrial civilization is not only for India but for the whole of humanity. A man is not necessarily happy because he is rich, or unhappy because he is poor.[32] The idea of simple life, sustainable development and appropriate technology are no mediaval fads but socio-scientific imperative of modern times. The Eco-Forum Report of Stockholm Conference on Environment, the Rio and the Copenhegan Conferences proclaim louder than Gandhi the urgency of a fresh look towards our industrial civilization, which is sick. Gandhi envisages a healthy civilization where there is progress with purity, development with creativity, prosperity with peace of mind.

Like technology, Gandhi fought the crudities of life with the weapon of science. His temper was nothing if not scientific. His whole life is "Experiments with Truth". He has "grown from truth to truth".[33] At the time of writing, he never think what he has said before. His aim is not to be consistent with his previous statements on a given question, but to be consistent with truth as it might present itself to me at a given moment. He has changed his views as the conditions had changed. His words and deeds have been dictated by prevailing conditions. There has been a gradual evolution in my environment and he reacted to it as a *Satyagrahi*.[34] He has been daily growing in the knowledge of *Satyagraha*. Thus Gandhi had a scientific attitude and temper. He says: "There is nothing like Gandhism. I do not like to leave a sect after me." He said: "The highest honour that my friends can do me is to enforce in their own lives the programne that I stand for or to resist me to their utmost if they do not believe in it.

Blind adoration, in the age of action is perfectly valueless, is often embarrassing and equality often painful".[35] This scientific attitude is reflected in vital matters of religion when he says (1) all religions are true; (2) all religions have some error in them; (3) all religions are almost as dear to me as my own Hinduism.[36] With the humility of a true scientist, he learnt to swim on the bosom of the ocean of Truth and reduce himself to a zero. As scientists are votaries after truth, so Gandhi after a continuous and relentless search after truth for 50 years came to the conclusion that truth is God. He was aware that millions have taken the names of God and in his name committed nameless cruelities. Hence it is safe to say that truth is God. So for a true scientist, Truth is his God.

However, Gandhi insisted that "scientific truths and discoveries should first of all cease to be mere instruments of greed.[37] He wanted science to be constructive. Besides, science should not help us in material existence but also in spiritual life. Mere science of matter is only a half way house. We must also explore the science of spirit. The dilemma of science is clear, it has brought immense benefits to mankind—plenty of foodstuffs, better health, more leisure, and near victory over space and time. On the other hand it has brought the world on the percipie of an atomic holocaust, dangerous problems of pollution, fast depletion of natural resources, alienation and depersonalization. Besides; there is poverty, inequality and torture in society. The dilemma of increasing military power and decreasing national security has no technical solution.[38] Hence what is needed is an integration of science and spirituality to overcome this crisis. We must not stop the progress of science but we must achieve it in an equilibrium between the inside and the outside.[39] Science, if it means "knowledge", it must include both knowledge of the outer and man's own nature. To quote Cyril Hinshewood, "To deny the reality of the inner world is a flat negation of all that is immediate in existence to minimise its significance is to depreciate the very purpose of living, and to explain it away as a product of natural selection is a plain fallacy.[40] We must salute the unwavering pursuit of science in the sense of cultivation of scientific spirit even with regard to the nature of man. It has highly been successful in the exploration of the outer world, but unfortunately not yet been applied adequately to the exploration of man's inner world. To Vinoba, therefore, science and spirituality should mean the same thing—one is more concerned with the outer space of the world, the other with the inner aspect. So he thinks that science and spirituality should combine not only to liberate India but the whole world.[41] This is the basis of global unity.

We need to stop the progress of science but if we want science to progress further, it must have a guide, which is the spiritual power. Science, in itself, is *amoral,* so it requires *values.* If it is wrongly guided, it will lead to unprecedented disaster and catastrophe. But if it is rightly guided, it will be the greatest boon for mankind. And this guidance will come from spirituality. Modern politics is dirt and a science of machination and murder & without ethics. But modern ethics is Hamlet like which delights to argue "To do or not to do".[42] Hence, unless we have faith in some absolute values, it will not serve us an adequate basis even for our moral actions. Solar age is the age of integration of science and spirituality where we have automatic strategy for unity of life. It is bound to reduce the disparity and monopoly of natural resources. So the visible trend of science is also towards unity and sanctity of life. A.N. Whitehead, therefore, says "that future of civilization depends on the degree to which we can balance the forces of science and religion".[43] Science will suffer grievously in its powers are not yoked to alleviate the suffering. But this direction will come from spirituality. Bertrand Russell rightly says that "we cannot give scientific justification for the goals that we might pursue or for the ethical principles that we adopt... No scientific reason can be given why it is bad to inflict wanton cruelty on one's fellows".[44] Science cannot supply us with an ethic.

This does not mean that we should became anti-science or anti-reason, which has no place in the affairs of man. It is untruth. But 'beyond reason' is not 'anti-reason' and 'beyond physics' is not 'anti -physics'. This "beyond empirical experience" is the hard core of religion or spirituality. Within the realm of science, there is no place for mysticism and there is the reign of reason is supreme. But the very kingdom of reason and human knowledge is an unfathomable mystery. But this mystery or mysticism is not scepticism or dogmatism, disbelief or superstition, it is acceptance of the limitation of the intellectual or conceptual knowledge. It does not reject para-intellectual experience. In fact, faith in the pursuit and value of science goes beyond science and reason and askin to religious feeling". Faith in science, faith in reason is not anti-reason, but beyond reason".[45] The current developments in quantum physics, cybernetics and molecular biology emphasise that the mystery is far deeper than ever thought before. It is one thing to say that we have no solution but altogether another thing to cavaliarily assert that there is no problem, no mystery.[46] The climax of ordinary consciousness is science. For yogic consciousness, we have to look into the realm of ESP or TK or intuitive knowledge.

Popularly, science and spirituality are regarded as opposed to each other. Science is objective, not subjective, hence to think of any purpose or goal for the universe is totally alien to science. Life is a synthesis of both science and spirituality. Science fulfils actions for our life, while spirituality provides a direction to our life. Hence Vinobaji says that "if spirituality is our vision, science is our strong feet".[47] We can fulfil our mission of life with the help of both. They are like two wings of a bird.[48] Science provides deep understanding of nature and the harmony it unfolds and beauty it unravels. It has also the immense power to transform society. But inspite of the dazzling triumphs of physical science, materialism proves itself always in the end a vain and helpless creed, and that too is why physical science itself with all its achievements, though it may accomplish comforts, can never achieve happiness and fullness for the human race.[49] Hence, science needs self-knowledge for guidance.

The moot question is how to make synthesis of science and spirituality. It is perhaps left to art and aesthetics, literature and intuition. From the moral point of view, both science and spirituality have got a remarkable sense of unity. As science is said to be neutral, impartial, without attachment and prejudice, so is true state of spirituality, where there is no envy, greed, jealousy, prejudices etc.[50] A truly spiritual man is a man of steadfast wisdom, who is above dualities of attachment and aversion, pleasure and pain, praise and blame. As scientific attitude is unful in all walks of life, so spiritual outlook is also of universal relevance. We badly need spiritualization of politics, economics, education, even commerce and military warfare.

Another point of unity between science and spirituality is that both are not opposed to religion. Science upholds truth and wants religion to rest on truth and real knowledge. Dogmatism is not religion, nor superstition is science. Einstein also says that the "foundation of morality or religion should not be dependent on myth nor tried to any authority best doubt about the myth or legitimacy about of the authority should imperil the foundation of sound judgement and action".[51] The scientific attitude to religion will cleanse it from dross of superstition and dogmatism. Similarly, spirituality too purifies religion because spirituality is the very core of religion. Vinobaji goes to the extent to say that the days of *religion* (sectarian and superstitious form) are over. As science should be distinguished from technology, so spirituality from "institutional religion". Unfortunately, spirituality has wrongly been associated with world-negating attitude and asceticism. Buddha's Theory of Transitoriness, Sankar's Theory of Maya, and general Indian theory of Moksa as escape from the cycles of life create on unfavourable attitude. But there is the concept of liberation *Jeevan mukti* while alive in flesh and blood, collective liberation (*Sarva-mukti*), the idea of *Bodhisattva* and the Fourfold ends (*Chatuh-Purusarthas*) are positive indications to correct the negative reflections. In India, the greatest spiritual figures like from Ram, Krishna, Janaka, Yagnavalkya, Mahavira, Buddha, Ramdas, to Vivekanand and Gandhi are shinning examples of spirituality in action. To Gandhi, God or salvation cannot be found into the caves of the Himalayas but here on earth in the true service of the lowliest and the lost. Hence Gandhi combines spirituality with social engineering and social dynamism. To him, life is a unity. We cannot divide it into watertight compartments. His whole life is truth in action. He even infused spirituality in his majestic struggle against imperialism and social-economic injustice he discovered Satyagraha as a moral-spiritual equivalent to the level of war. Global crisis is both inner as well as outer. In the inner field, there is the crisis of perception, in the outer field, the crisis is the conditioning of human psyche working as a single channel computer resulting in lowering the level of perception, sensitivity and rationality. The old chasm between *knowledge* and *wisdom* has widened dangerously.[52] In our thirst for knowledge, we have cut ourselves from wisdom. The contemporary western civilization is still rooted in Cartesian dualistic metaphysics and subject-object dualism. From mind-matter dualism we have developed space-time matrix. But we have forgotten Einstein's warning that "space-time does not claim existence of its own, but only structural quality of the field".[53] In our pride of science, we have come to despise and reject intuitive and instinctual perceptions that have heretofore animated and given perspective and hope and meaning to human existence. David Bohm's physics requires a new instrument of thought and perception of the "unbroken wholeness" in a non-dual frame which can understand life and in a concrete manner, rather than in the abstract, linear terms. The subject-object dualistic mode of intellectual knowledge has its own limitations. It cannot understand the deeper level of mind-brain interaction. Max Born feels that "clever, rational ways of thinking are not enough".[54] Hence it has no cure for psychological imbalances. "The world-view implied by modern physicist is inconsistent with our society which does not reflect harmonious interrelatedness we observe in nature"[55] says Fritzof Capra. It means we need an inward revolution. Hence it is fime to say good bye to time-hallowed distinction between subject and objects. Though we have to accept dualism in everyday practical life, we have to give it up on philosophical plain. Hence Schordinger concludes : "world is given to me only once, not one existing and one perceived. Subject and object are only one. The present dualistic knowledge mechanism is to bifurcate the 'seer' and the 'seen' is mutilation of knowledge and is only one-sided and partial knowledge,[56] and "which leads to an argument between nature and man".[57] We need an understanding which is the immediate, the present, always timeless, psychologically flowering and without interferences. This is quantum jump from symbolic dualistic frame to non dual frame, from fragmentation to holistic or ecological perception. This is intuition, which is not against reason but beyond reason. Discovering in the field of atomic physics do recognise the insufficiency and inadequacy of subject-object dualistic intellectual knowledge. Here, we have to recognize the limitation of 'scientific knowledge' and devise a different method of knowledge, which is the basis of spirituality.

Conclusion

There is greater relevance of the synthesis of science and spirituality for global unity. Nationalism and even institutional religion are too week instruments for such thing. Nationalism in one sense is another form of tribalism and institutional religion are not only assuming aggressive postures against each other but also creating many confusions . The movement of modern knowledge called science has eroded the foundations from which norms could be derived: it has destroyed the very idea of norm as such. First it was nature that was "neutralized" with respect to value then *man* himself. Now we shiver in the nackedness of nihilism in which near omnipotence is paired with near emptiness, greatest capacity with knowing least for what ends to use it. Hence we badly need an ethics to cope with the extreme powers which we possess today and which are constantly increasing. Moral neutrality with ethics and spirituality cannot meet the demand of the ethics of the future. The present state of western culture and society gives a tragic spectrum of the beginning of the disintegration of their Sensate Super-system. Wisdom has faded we are satisfied with small intellectual horizons. But this is not only true with the West, it is also largely but pathetically true of India. India today, perhaps is more materialist than the west. Hence if India is to strive for global unity, it must work for synthesis of Science and spirituality in thought, word, action and organs.

REFERENCES

1. Prof. Delisle Burns, *Preface* to the New Edition, *Hind Swaraj* by M.K. Gandhi, Ahmedabad: Navajivan Publishing House 1958 (Reprinted), p. 7. Burns reproduced a dialogue where Gandhiji replying to a question "whether he was against *all* machinery", Gandhiji said : "How can I be when I know that even this body is a most delicate piece of machinery... What I object to is a *craze* for machinery, not machinery as such... Take the case of a Singer's Sewing Machine. It is one of the few useful things ever invented", when asked "But there would have to be factory for making these sewing machines and power driven machinery", Gandhiji in reply said : "Yes. But I am socialist enough to say that such factories should be nationalized, State controlled." *Ibid.*

2. Gandhi, M.K., *Hind Swaraj,* Ahmedabad: Navajivan Publishing House, Rev. New Edition, 1939, Reprinted 1958, p. 93.

3. *Ibid.*, p. 94.

4. *Ibid.*, p. 96.

5. *Ibid.*

6. Gandhi, M.K., *Complete Works of M. Gandhi,* New Delhi, Govt. of India, Vol. 16, pp. 134-5.

7. C.W., Vol. 22, pp. 101-2.

8. C.W., Vol. 25, pp. 251-52.

9. C.W., Vol. 47, pp. 89-90.

10. C.W., Vol. 48, p. 353.

11. C.W., Vol. 58, p. 400.

12. C.W., Vol. 61, p. 416.

13. C.W., Vol. 64, p. 148.

14. C.W., Vol. 71, p. 383.

15. C.W., Vol. 82, pp. 132-33.

16. C.W., Vol. 85, pp. 239-40.

17. C.W., Vol. 87, p. 249.

18. Rajkrishna, *Human Values and Technological Change,* Kashi: A.B. Sarva Seva Sangh Prakashan, 1958, p. 5.

19. Rolt, L.T.C., "Science Run Mad", *Aryan Path,* Bombay, March 1956, p. 115.

20. Huxley, Aldous, *Science, Liberty and Peace,* p. 23.

21. Rajkrishna, *Ibid.,* p. 91.

22. Ropke, W., *Civitas Humana,* pp. 161-62.

23. Low, A.M., *Science in Industry,* p. 148, quoted by Rajkrishna, *Ibid.,* p. 11.

24. Humford, Lewis, *Condition of Man,* p. 309 (Statement attributed to Pope Pias XI).

25. "Industrialism and Happiness", Report prepared by J.C. Hunt, *Aryan Path,* April 1956, p. 167.

26. Scott and Lynton, *The Community Factor in Modern Technology,* UNESCO Publications, pp. 29-30.

27. Pal, Lesile, "The Effect of Technology", *The Hibbert Journal,* Oct. 1956, pp. 26-33.

28. Paisod, M., "The Challenge of Totalitarianism', *New Leader,* May 7, 1956.

29. Pandey, S., 'The Ultra-Modern Gandhi", *Gandhi Marg,* April 1982, p. 23.

30. *Ibid.,* p. 23.

31. Galbraith, J.K., *The New Industrial State.* p. 19.

32. Gandhi, M.K., *Hind Swaraj,* p. 61.

33. Gandhi, M.K., *Harijan*, 30.3.39.

34. *Young India*, 12.6.24.

35. Gandhi, M.K., *Sabarmati*, Report of the 1st Annual Meeting of the Federation of International Fellowships, 13-15th Jan., 1928.

36. Gandhi, M.K., *Young India*, 13.11.24.

37. Kothari, D.S., "Science and Humanism", Delhi University *Convocation Address*, 16.4.1983, p. 9.

38. Indrasen (ed.), *Science and Culture*, Pondichery, Sri Aurobindo Ashram, 1951, p. 114.

39. Presidential Address, Royal Society of London, 1962.

40. *Science and Spirituality: An Exploration*, Varanasi: Sarva Seva Sangh, p. 19.

41. *Ibid.*, p. 21.

42. Kothari, D.S., *Some Thoughts on Science and Religion*, New Delhi, 1977, p.2.

43. *Ibid.*, p. 3.

44. Warner, Heisenberg, *Physics and Beyond: Enconters and Conversations*, Harper & Row, 1971.

45. Kothari, D.S., *Some Thoughts on Science and Religion*, pp. 5-6.

46. *Science and Spirituality: An Exploration*, pp. 50-51.

47. Bhave, V., *Atma Janana Aur Vignan*, Kasi, S.S. Sangh Prakashan, 1964, p. 93.

48. *Ibid.*

49. Indrasen, *Ibid.*

50. Bhave, V., *Teesri Shakti*, Varanasi: Sarva Seva Sangh, 1969, p. 4.

51. Quoted by D.S. Kothari, "Science and Ahimsa Centre", Inaugural Speech, Ahmedabad, 6.4.1983.

52. Singh, S., *The Human Survival,* Chandigarh: Faith Publishers, 1993, p. 1.

53. Einstein, A., *Reality: The Special and the General Theory*(Trans), New York: R.W. Lawson, 15th ed. 1961, pp. 155-56.

54. Max Born, quoted in Hindeki Yakuwa's *Creativity and Intuition,* Tokyo: Physics Today, 1969, Vol. 22, p. 53.

55. Fritzof Capra, *The Tao of Physics,* New York: Banton Books, 1988 (2nd ed.), p. 298.

56. Brown, G. Spencer, *Laws of Nature,* New York, Julian Press, 1972, pp. 104-05.

57. Heisenberg, A., in Ken Wilber, *The Spectorum of Consciousness,* New York, Julian Press, 1972, p. 104-5.

Chapter 10

THE AFRICAN LEGACY OF NON-VIOLENCE

After spending almost 21 years, Gandhi had left South Africa on 18th July 1914. When he sailed he wrote—"I have left South Africa but not my connection with that country". On 28th June 1946, at his prayer meeting he said: "He was born in India but was made in South Africa". In a letter to Dr. Dadoo and Mr. G.M. Naicker, two freedom fighters from South Africa, he said : ' Truly speaking it was after I went to South Africa for 20 years that I became what I am now. My love for South Africa and my concern for her problems are no less than for India". In his prayer meeting held at Pune on 10th July 1946, recognising the debt, Gandhi says : "In a way I belong to South Africa having passed twenty years of the best part of life there." Only two days of his martyrdom, becoming extremely emotional, Gandhi observed; "I have myself lived in South Africa for 20 years and I can say that it is my country".

Apart from these emotional attachment to Africa, Gandhi had many gifts both ideological and relating to his programmes. Here he had became convinced of the invincibility of non-violent resistance to evil, which is called by the name of *Satyagraha* (*Satya*—Truth; *Agraha* = holding fast *i.e.*, holding fast to truth). Gandhi used the term "passive resistance" in describing it. Even Gandhi did not quite understand the implications of "passive resistance" as he called it. As the struggle advanced, the phrase gave rise to confusion and it appeared shameful to permit this great struggle to be known only by an English name.

As that foreign phrase could hardly pass a current coin among the çommunity. A small prize was announced in *Indian Opinion* and the competitors for the prize had fairly sufficient material. Sri Maganlal Gandhi was one of the competitors and he suggested the word '*Sadagraha*' meaning "firmness in a good cause". Gandhi liked the word, but it did not fully present the whole idea he wished to connote. He therefore corrected it to "*Satyagraha*" *Satya* (Truth) implies love and *Agraha* (firmness) engenders as a synonym for force. He thus began to call his movement *Satyagraha*. Thus Gandhi owes to African not only regard the original and evolution of his unique method of non-violent social action but he also ows its name to South Africa. Incidentally, Gandhi's greatest gift to humanity is the discovery of this weapon of non-violent mass action. Today, in this age of stockfile of atomic arsenels, if we cannot abolish war, war will abolish us. Hence the use of "moral equivalent of war" is not 'religious fad' but a scientific compulsion. Infact, war has lost its dynamics. Hence, search for an equivalent of war is certain. Non-violence is neither an ethical dogma, or a religious virtue, it is inevitable for the world. The great scientist and inventor of atom bomb, Dr. Einstein when asked here shall be fight the "Third World War", he said "I do not know about the Third World War but we shall fight in the Fourth World War with our fists and hands." It means that the present method of warfare has become out of date, self-suicidal, anti-man and even anti-science. We have also seen the successful demonstration of this method of non-violent mass action not only in the emancipation of Indian sub-continent from the yoke of the biggest world imperial power but has shown Martin Luther King's victory against racial discrimination in USA, humbling the might of military Communist dictatorship in Poland under the leadership of Leh Walesa and restoration of democracy in the great Soviet Union. There are other examples also. Fighting injustice with traditional method of violence has become both theoretical wrong and practically unproductive simply because the modern state, thanks to science and technology, has became more powerful than even the *Leviathan,* hence spoardic fight with arms and ammunition are liable to be crushed by the state power. While if the non-violent struggle is crushed, its receives wider sympathy and support and if is not crushed, it goes on growing from step to step. Hence, the method of non-violent mass-action is more relevant today than at the time of Socrates, Jesus and Galelio. Infact, resistance to injustice through non-violent method is not new in human history. Gandhi's contribution lies in transforming this individual action into a scientific social action. Richard Gregg in his book on "The Power of Non-Violence", Joan Von Durant in his A Study of Revolution" Martin Luther King in his *Stride Towards Freedom* and many western thinkers have acknowledged that the method of fighting injustice with non-violent method is not only civilizationally appropriate but is the only practical way left to us. Even looked from theoretical angle, if "revolution" means "sudden and fundamental change" of ideas and ideals, values and ethos, they cannot be changed under duress or by physical external force. Rather, force or violence leads to counter-violence which never ends. The world has witnessed enough the horrors of counter-revolution and consequent debasement of human values. Hence we can say that "the more of violence, the less of revolution". Buddha, Jesus and other saints and seers did change the face of humanity without shedding a drop of human blood or generating hatred and animosity. It is why it is more lasting and much less counter-productive. Hence, I am constrained to say that

Africa became the first laboratory of a non-violent mass action which is bound to be the faith of the 21st Century.

Secondly, Africa's second gift to the world through Gandhi is the experiment of "non-racial democracy". We have seen the horrible results of 'racial polity' in the forms of Nazism in Germany, Facism in Italy, and in South Africa. The pernicious doctrine of "Whitemen's burden" is flagrant violation of human dignity and human rights. In history, racism and imperialism as well as negation of democracy go together. No doubt, Gandhi true to his Indian legacy of multi-racial and multi-religious harmonious nationalism of the land of his birth starting from his family and neighbourhood but again the credit goes to the sacred soil of South Africa, which provided Gandhi to learn object lessons in fighting racism from the beginning. While supporting the petition of the coloured people in 1906, he said: "The petition is non-Indian in character, although British Indian, being coloured people are very largely affected by it. Likewise therefore, the Indian and non-Indian sections of coloured communities should and do, remain apart, and have the separate organisations, there is no doubt that each can give strength to the other in urging their common rights." (*Indian Opinion*, 14.3.1906). Mr. Swan has most uncharitably accused Gandhi of being "racial purist" and being proud of his race quoting Gandhi out of context :" "we believe as much in the purity of race as we think they (Europeans) believe as much in purity of race as we think." This statement of Gandhi was actually made in the context of the white fears of mass Indian immigration. Gandhi infact was fearing of white fears of misageneration between themselves and Indian. Here "they" mean *Whites* and not Africans. Another western writer, L.M. Thompson accused Gandhi as being "the advocate of the interests of local elite, merchants, traders and western educated white colored workers". This is also not based on facts. Gandhi chose issues that could unite rather than divide the community. For example, for positive action, he chose the famous "Franchise Issue" and negatively, he eshewed the issue of *Gold Law* which concerned only the merchant class. Thompson's charge that Gandhi had scarcely any contact with the educated Africans as he was personally influenced by the anti-African racism, is unjust. Similarly, Robert Johnson's accusation of Gandhi of making disparging remarks to Africans on the failure of Indian Passive Resistance is again a dishonest way of quoting Gandhi out of context. To put the record straight, it is true Gandhi said "How this race which is second to none in the world would in point of physical strength, is so timid that a Negro is afraid at sight of a European child". But in the full context Gandhi had said: "The Negroes will acquainted with the use of spear, the bow and the arrow stood in mortal terror of the whites who weilded the gun in which no match is needed, nothing more has to be done beyond moving the finger". This shows the high appreciation of the valor and heroic nature of the Africans. Gandhi is also accused of imbibing some of the prejudices of the white toward Indian community and using the word "Kaffir" until 1908 to describe the Africans and denouncing the "Zulus" as "very lazy" who will with difficulty work at a stretch for 6 months. On the otherhand Gandhi has said: "*Natives have as much right to Franchise as the Indians or the Whites*". *Times of Natal* (26.10.1894) published a letter from Gandhi : 'The Indians do not regret that capable natives can exercise the franchise. They would regret if it were otherwise. The Indian however asserts that they too, if capable, should have the right. You in your wisdom, could not allow the Indian or the native the precious privilege under any circumstances because they have a dark skin." Gandhi's own account reveals extreme sympathy for the Zulus when they were wounded and left uncared and in the most inhuman way transgressing the rules of war. Gandhi nursed them. Gandhi recounts his experience: "Zulus would not talk to us but from the gestures and expressions of their eyes, they see and feel as if God had sent us to their sccur." (Doke, J. *M.K. Gandhi,* Ahmedabad, Navajivan Prakashan, p. 1120. Similarly, a charge that Gandhi did not favour joint action with Africans is palpably wrong and mischievous and motivated. Gandhi considered these two indigenous groups as sons of the soil whose rights were to prevail over the interests of Indians and Whiles, both being immigrants. He had practical reasons of reorganising this separate identity—first to recognise them as 'sons of the soil" and secondly to ward off any allegation by the then while rulers that Indians were inciting the Blacks, which gave the rulers handle to commit slavery and indiscriminate deportation of Indians.

These are expressions of support by non-white organisations to the Indian cause and in turn the Indians supported their demands. Hat stronger proof of Gandhi's solidarity with the Blacks can be than his big and unequivocal support in 1906 to the Petition of the Coloured. Gandhi contacted not only with the educated but more with the non-educated Africans because for him, the Last Man is the object of his prayer. Gandhi is said to have openly said: "Rubusana (a representative of Blacks) can sit under provincial Council but not in the Union Cabinet is a glaring anomaly . John Tengo Jabavu's effort to establish college and Gandhi exhorted not only the Indians there but the British Indians to learn from the example of self-sacrifice (CWMG, 8.235). No doubt Gandhi accepted administrative differentiation but not legislative discrimination.

He had identified with the aspirations of the majority and abandoning their exclusiveness. Even Indian question were deliberately subordinated to the larger question of democracy and equality. He had waged a war against the

Black Act, which applied to the Chinese as well as to the Indians whom they therefore joined in the Satyagraha struggle, though each community worked through its own organization. Even the Chinese were in high spirits when arrests commenced. So as the case even in the heterogenous Indian community consisting of Gujrati and Tamilian, Hindus and Muslims not only this, Gandhi got support from a number of eminent European like *Mr. Albert West,* who was not only a vegetarian friend of Gandhi but who also worked with Gandhi to nurse the patients of fatal disease of plague in Johannesburg and helped in publishing his journal for his struggle. He also participated in his Ashram activities in Phoenix. He had taken over the whole management of the Ashram which many members of the Ashram were in Jail and also managed the press and paper. The second notable European friend was Mr. Ritch was the moving spirit of the South African British Indian Committee in London. The third was Mr. Polak who had left the sub-editorship of the *Transval Critic* to join the staff of *Indian Opinion.* Though the Polaks did not see eye to eye with Gandhi in the Non-Cooperation Movement, his services to India is exemplary. Next to Mr. Polak was a German Mr. Hermann Kallenbach whose sense of solidarity and support was almost exemplery. He was most faithful personal emissary of Gandhi for very crucial contact. His sacrifice for Gandhi's struggle for South African struggle is unique. So war Miss Sonja Schlesian whose single mind devotion to work in South Africa is unparalled. She had sacrificed all for the Indian cause without expecting any reward whatever. Miss Dick also was a picture of loyalty and purity. Herbert Kitchen worked with the Boer War and for sometime was editor of the *Indian Opinion.* Even in Transval, Gandhi had many sympathises and friends for his movement like Mr. Hosken, ex-President of the Association of Chambers of Commerce of South Africa and a member of Legislative Assembly of the Transval, Mr. Albert Cartwright, Rev. Charles Phillips, Mr. Vere Stent etc. assisted him in the struggle against racial discrimination. Even among the European ladies like Miss Hobbouse, Miss Olive Schreiner, Miss Molteno also joined Gandhi in his movement against Black Act and colar bar. Infact, the struggle in South Africa had united all races.

True Gandhi had repeatedly accepted administrative differentiation but not legislative discrimination, because administrative discrimination can be to removed but statutory discrimination would be more difficult to remove. Gandhi believed that the European apprehension over being swamped by Asiatics was shown to be misplaced, if they were persuaded so accordingly than civilizational and cultural standards of India and if the Indians increasingly adapted themselves to the Western standards of life, the quest for equality with the Whites would be nearer.

So far South Africa is concerned, till 1914, there was accommodation and compromise, since 1914, there was resistance and challenges to racial discrimination policy of the Government. This was firstly because of urbanization and increasing of proletatrisation of Indian workers. So *Industrial Conciliation Act 1924* did not exclude Indian as it did with Africans. The number of organised Indian workers grew from 12600 in 1934 to 26400 in 1939. Then there was rapid growth of education. In 1927 there were 53 schools and 9776 pupils which rose to 102 Schools and 22294 in 1936. The report of Brown Commission says that only 50% of children got admission. Then were Anti-Segregation Council in Natal and the Natal based groups in Transval. There were interactions with the working class and there was growing consciousness and awareness among the South Africa born Indians. From the Right to Domicile, they demanded

Right to Full Citizenship. In 1927, Natal Indian Vigilance Association had challenged the government and last but not the least Govt. of India had shown serious concern over repatriation of Indians born in this country.

So under the leadership of Mahatma Gandhi, South Africa was gradually entering a new era, the era of non-racial democracy. Though ethnicity will continue to cast its shadow on politics, as religion and castes do in India even after four decades of secular democracy. The fruition and fulfilment of this non-racial democracy has been under Dr. Nelson Mandela and Mr. Kirk when South African struggle for democracy and equality, Indian abandoned their exclusiveness and identified with aspirations of the majority. Thanks to the advent of national Government in India the Indian question was deliberately subordinated to the larger question of democracy and equality in South Africa.

It has been often charged that "Indians in South Africa were never a people but have always been a 'problem', in "a question" (Violet Witherall, *The Indian Question,* Capetown, 1946). But the learned author knows that the (Indians) were an issue even before any one of them landed in Natal, the first home in South Africa. For example, as early as 1854, the Governor of Cape (then Natal was a part of Cape Colony) responding to the demand of Cape Colonialists, the majority of whom were of British stock, suggested *import of Indian labour* to improve the colony's economy on the pattern of Mauritus. When there was a charter to Natal in 1856, opposition to Indianise as 'suicidal policy' was placed, elected members opposed but planters interest got the proposal accepted in 1859. Hence the first batch of coolies (Indian indentured labour) came on October 12, 1860. Between 1860-1911, there was steady stream of Indian labour immigration into Natal with a total of 152184 workers, men and women.

In 1875, *Protection of Indian Immigrants Act* was approved at the instance of His Majesty's Govt. Hence Indian immigrants were not as a "temporary expedient" but as a permanent problem. White dominated colony had no room for Indians except as part of the labour force. There was grant of land also to them. Indian labour was not only industrious but also enterprising. By 1880, more than 20 thousands ex-indentured labour had settled down. All in all, the Indian presence was forbidding.

International Impact of South African Struggle for Liberation

On 8th January 1982 at the occasion of 70th Anniversary of the founding of African National Congress, Mr. Anthony Sampson observed: "It is a Congress around which African opposition and its allies have centered for the last ten years and it is Congress which is likely to present the main threat to white supremacy in the future." It is to be noted that the impact of South African struggle has not been static. It has changed the world situation. The Great Sharpvelli Massacre of 1960 and the Student Uprising of 1976 had clearly triggered responses at U.N. for decades and ultimately humbling down the minority ethnic white rule in South Africa. But the ground work was done by Gandhi. This campaign against racial discrimination in South Africa also inspired such a successful non-violent struggle in USA under the leadership of Martin Luther king, who had a Gandhian heritage and strategy. So Andrew Young, the then USA permanent representative to U.N. Special Committee on Aparthied in February 1978 said: "To put an end to aparthied in Africa, we are also putting an end to aparthied in America". Addressing rally in Madison Square Garden. Robson, fervently hoped that "the movement for *racial justice* in U.S. was strengthened by support for South African Struggle..." In the process of helping others, we add to our own strength and bring nearer full freedom for ourselves." Addressing a meeting of Human Rights Day in 1965 at Hunter College, New York, Martin Luther King said: "The civil rights movement in USA has derived immense inspiration from successful struggle of those Africans who have obtained freedom in their own nations." If we look back, between 1940-1950, Afro-Asian Group was formed at the U.N. and there definite and concerted campaigns of Defiance against Unjust Laws. Freedom Charter of 1955 was the result in which the historic statement comes : 'we the people in South Africa believe that South Africa belongs to all who live in it—black and white.' Addressing at the receiving Nobel Peace Prize, Chuf Lutuli said : "We South Africans understand that much as others might do for us, our freedom cannot come to us a gift from abroad. Our freedom we must make ourselves'. Hearing this, Gandhi's similar words resounds: "*Swaraj* can never be a gift by one nation to another. It is a treasure to be purchased with nation's best blood.' (*Young India*, 5.1.1922).

EPILOGUE

1. Satyagraha

If Gandhian gift to Africa is great, African gift to Gandhi is still greater. Gandhi was no doubt, born in India but became a prophet of non-violent mass action only in South Africa. Hence his *Satyagraha* is not an Indian import to Africa but veritably an African ideological export not only to India but world at large. Gandhi's book on *Satyagraha in South Africa* is a vivid testimony to it. According to Gandhi, the term *Satyagraha* was invented and employed in connection therewith... and this was the first attempt to apply the principle of Satyagraha to politics on a large scale..." (Preface to *Satyagraha in South Africa,* M.K. Gandhi, Ahmedabad, Navajivan Press, p. XI). Gandhi minus Satyagraha cannot be conceived.

2. Constructive Programme

Satyagraha has two dimensions—agitational as we find in the forms of strikes, Non-cooperation, Civil Disobedience etc. but the other dimension of Satyagraha is various Constructive Programmes like communal and religious harmony, removal of aparthied, village uplift, relevant education and so on. We find that Gandhi had learnt object lessons in all such programmes in South Africa. He had established Phoenix Ashram and Tolstoy Farm, where there was an exercise in collective life, simple life-style and dignity of labour etc. When Gandhi came to India, he drew 18 Constructive Programmes but their genesis lie in the sacred soil of Africa.

3. Ethical Life and Vows of Life

The virtues of non-violence, truth, celebacy etc. are no doubt rooted in Indian religious heritage but their practice in personal life of Mahatma Gandhi found fruition in South Africa. The entire non-violent resistance movement in South Africa—from protest and petition to bonfire of certificates, facing the charge of horses without retaliation, imprisonment, crossing the border, the great march, facing the government policy of blood and iron, firing and so on are epics of non-violent struggle. This led to Gandhi to start Satyagraha after Satyagraha—Viramgam, Bambay, Champaran, Ahmedabad, kheda, struggle against Rowlatt Act, Khilafat, etc. It is proved that non-violence is not a cloistered virtue but something practical and useful for life. Gandhi had learnt to observe the vows of non-violence (love) truth and even practice of celebacy (including married *Brahmacharya*), non-possession in his personal life in South Africa.

4. Religious Pluralism

We know that there were men and women of many religions—Hindus, Muslims, Christians, Zorastrians, Jews and so on. Ofcourse, Gandhi had learnt the lessons of religious tolerance in his family and in his neighbourhood and through his own religious scriptures. But South Africa provided a working laboratory for the practice of religious harmony. To him all religions are true but he also believed that every religions have some faults or weaknesses. But there is essential unity of all religions. Hence he did not believe in proselytisation on conversion. A true Hindu is a true Christian and so on. To Gandhi, religious harmony became an article of faith, which he practised through out his life in India. His religion was ethical religion. He would reject all authority if it conflicts with reason and morality.

5. Indian Aparthied

Gandhi's fight against racialism in South Africa was epic in character. When he went to India, he carried this heritage and put abolition of untouchability in the forefront in the course of Indian Freedom Struggle. He led a crusade against "touch me not' ism of a section of hindus by the other section. To him untouchability is not only not a part and parcel of Hinduism but a plague. He led temple entry of these socially outcastes people, lived amongst them, did a lot for their improvement in education, sanitation etc.

6. Basic Education

Like Socrates, Gandhi was an ideal teacher. But he did not think that literacy alone in education. On the otherhand according to him, literacy is neither the beginning or end of education. It requires around development of hand, head and heart. Hence, he started schools in South Africa for Indian settles but it was unique. Like Montessori, he believed in "learning by doing". This is similar to Dewey's 'work-experience' or Makrenko's emphasis on work, or Mao's experiment of "half-half". Gandhi borrowed his experience of South Africa to his experiments in education in India.

7. Journalism

Gandhi started his journalist career in South Africa, which he carried to India. He published *Indian Opinion* in South Africa in English, Gujrati, Hindi and Tamil. But the Hindi and Tamil sections were eventuality discontinued. *Indian Opinion* played an important role in the Satyagraha struggle in South Africa. After premature death of Mansukhlal Nazar, Herbet Kitchin, Henry Polak etc. helped him. He set a moral standard of the paper by not accepting advertisements even it meant considerable hardship. When he came to India he carried this legacy of journalism as a potent weapon of mass-education and social change. He started *Young India, Navajivan Harijan, Harijan Sevak* and they brought renaissance in the country. However to him, the aim of journalism should be service, to understand the popular feeling and give expression to it; to arouse among the people certain desirable sentiments, and fearlessly to expose popular defects. Seeds of such moral and social journalism has South Africa legacy.

Chapter 11

SVA-RAJYA VS SVĀ-RAJYA

1. Concept & Context

Sva-rajya is a multi-dimensional and dynamic concept in Indian thought and culture. It is at once a metaphysical, moral, political and cultural concept. Hence, there have been many interpretations as well as misunderstandings about it. Historically, it is clearly derived from the Vedic vocabulary as one of the eight types of polity as listed in the Aitreya Brahman[1] of the Rgveda. However, the term used is *Svā-rajyam* instead of *Sva-rājyam*. However, in the Rgveda text itself, the term *Sva-rajye* has been used as a purely value concept—Vyachiste Bahupayyai Yatemahi Sva-rajye.[2] The Brahmanas provide historical records about the prevalence of the eight types of polity in different parts of India or abroad. However the characteristic feature of the vedic polity is its cosmic outlook. Instead of having fractured concept of 'nation-States', they had a universal and totalistic concept of polity—Kindgom of the entire Earth—spread to the limitless ocean. There is only one polity as they recognised that the human family is one—Vasudhaiva Kutumbakam. They had only one ambition to see to entire humanity with the greatest nobility—*Kranvanto viswam aryam.* This should not be understood as an utterance of the sense of false vanity or national pride but an innocent desire for a global community and a global family, at best an expression of cultural nationalism, never interested in any political domination or world-conquest. There is an Aryan Constitution, no doubt, but it was never imposed. Domination upon others, either political or religious has not been in the Indian psyche from its antiquity—of Treta Era where Rama handed over the kingdom of Lanka to Ravana or in modern time B'desh to its rightful rulers. So also religious conversion as an institution not found favourable to our taste and temperament. Hence, even the concept of an Empire (*Sāmarajyam*) is not associated with geographical extension or annexation but only cultural and spiritual fraternity.

2. Sva-Rajya vs. Svā-rajya

Both 'Sva-rajya' and *Svā-rajya*' are derived from the same Vedic vocabulary and sound so similar that Sva-rājya is itself identified with *Svā-rajya*—Sva-rājyameva eva Svā-rājyam'. But if we go beyond this Semantic semblances, they suggest two different values of polity, morality and metaphysices. 'Sva-rājya' literally means 'Self-rule' or Self-Government' where as *Svā-rājya*' transcending political dimension suggests ethical dimensions like 'self-control' or going beyond to the metaphysical realm equating Svā-rājya with 'Self-conquest', Self-knowledge' and 'Freedom of the Self'. While *'Sva-rājya'* lays emphasis upon one's *rights, 'Svā-rajya'* emphasises upon *duties* and obligation. Hence, purity of means, righteousness and sanctity of human personality are the values attached to its. Any ambition for power through untruth, injustice and violence is unknown and unacceptable. Hence, duty or dharma is the characteristic feature of Swāraj-polity. Incidently, "civilization is that mode of conduct which points out to man the path of duty. Performance of duty and observance of morality are convertible terms. To observe morality is to attain mastery over our mind and our passions"[3] —says Gandhi. In fact, this *'Self-rule'* is the essence of *Svarajya*. "The true source of rights is duty".

If we all discharge our duties, rights will not be far to seek. If leaving duties unperformed we run after rights, they will escape us like a will-o-the wisp".[4] This is the philosophy behind *Dharma* also. Dharma enjoins upon us to do our duties. The Gita also proclaims : "Action alone is thy province, never the fruits thereof".[5] One may criticise that this idea means "all absence of purpose". But, this ethics of selfless action or duty for duty sake as to be understood in a proper metaphysical context of *Self-realization* of *Freedom*. Nothing matters except the goodwill, the willing fulfilment of the purpose of God. Tolstoy explain better in "what I believe" - "The belief in a remuneration of work rests on the assumption that we have a claim to something, but man has no rights and can have none. He is ever in debt for the welfare given him and therefore can make no demands on any one".[6] So does the Holy Quroan says : My wage is concern of Allah only.[7] Unto Allah belongeth the sequel of all things.[8] To be detached is never to abandon action. It means only that "there should be no selfish purpose behind our actions".[9] This is therefore a devise known as *Sva-dharma* has been introduced to appreciate and cling to our own duty (Sva-dharma) though imperfectly carried out than the duty of others well performed. Even in practical life and usage, no people have risen who thought only of rights. Only those did so who thought of duties. A man may give up his right, but he may not give up his duty without being guilty of a grave dereliction. Duty is therefore inescapable without sustaining moral injury. Hence Gandhi says that Swaraj would be real Swaraj when there would be no occasion for safeguarding rights.[10] Thus it may be equated with the *Ram-Rajya* or the kingdom of God on Earth, where everybody is conscious of one's duty. Naturally, the attention is towards one's own self, Self-introspection, and Self-purification. Hence hankering after rights and their misuse through arrogance of power do not create problems in the state of Svā-rājya. Alvin Toffler in his *Power-Shift* deals about the "Crescendoing struggles for power".[11] The use of violence as a source of power will not disappear and the control of immense wealth will continue to confer enormous power on them.[12] Hence a *Power-shift*, if at all is necessary, it has to be towards acquiring moral and spiritual power. Eqivalent of violence has to be found in love and non-violence and for all this, what is needed is a "Goodness Politics" [13] (Jaya Prakash Narain) or "Higher Politics" or "*Religious Politics*"[14] (Karl Jaspers) of a self-revealing man that can rescue us from political crises.

In this regard, the Vedic concept of Sva-rājya is found to lay emphasis upon moralisation and spiritualisation of politics.[15] For this, the Vedas suggests two criteria - (1) Universality (Vyachista) and (2) Popular Sanction (Vahu-Pāyye). If politics lacs universality, it is most likely to degenerate into communalism, casteism, linguism, regionalism and so on. Sectarianism in politics is at the root of all political conflicts. It reduces politics into a ladder for unscrupulous seizure of power. Politics should mean "brotherhood", which is a branch of ethics. The second condition of Svā-rajya is popular sanction (Vahu-Pāyye) through a politics of democratic concensus. Hence, the Vedic Svā-rajya is neither a kind of aristocracy or oligarchy-based upon superiority of any caste or colour, nor it is a 'theocratic' system, nor even a 'dictatorship of the proletariate' because there is revolutionary change in its decision-making process making it based on unanimity (*Sarva-Sammati*) or near-unanimity (*Sarvānumati*) or through widest possible consensus. Vinoba Bhave is also critical of the method of the present "quantitative democracy" which in its worst form is reduced to "fifty one as against forty-nine," and instead advocates to accept the principle of conciliation (Panchayat), where "God is said to speak through all the five persons constituting the

Board of conciliation or Panchayat. This means that a truly democratic decision must reach the common mind and avoiding structural Balkanisation of the people at the grass-root level.

3. Svā-rajya and value-Integral

No doubt *Sva-rajya* is a Vedic term which literally means 'rule over one's own self". Its original connotation signified autonomy of the moral-self with self-control. Government over self is the truest *Swaraj*, it is synonymous with *Moksha* or Salvation. Out of this moral and spiritual meanings, political meaning has also been derived right from the time of the Vedas, as Vedic polity is highly based on the moral and spiritual values of *Svā-rajya*. However, since life is unity and not a water-tight compartment in Indian thought, Swāraj has also an integral character. It is at once moral and political, cultural and spiritual. Knowledge, righteousness and polity have been so well integrated that despotism of one-class over the others are automatically avoided.[16] Even the king has to abide to the dictates of law and righteousness. If this balance is lost, and there is unbriddled freedom to one section of society, nation itself meets with disaster. (*Rastrameva Visyahanti*).[17] There has been strong moral and spiritual basis of polity in the Vedic literature.[18] Hence, polity is called as the duty of polity (Raj-dharma).[19]

There has been inherent vitality and dynamism in the concept of *Sva-rajya*, so inspite of its great antiquity which is traced into the Vedas and the Upanisads, it has been fully alive like a living idea. We can find its vibrations in the writings of almost all the leaders of modern Indian Renaissance like Swami Dayanand, Swami Vivekanand, Sri Aurobindo and others. However, it acquired its political significance during our freedom movement. Dadabhai Naroji, was the first stateman who made open demand for *Swaraj* in 1906 from the platform of the Indian National Congress and later on it was popularised by Bal Gangadhar Tilak, Sri Aurobindo, Annie Besant etc. But the concept of *Swaraj* as conceived by Gandhi assumed an action-programme of the masses based on the ideology of *Hind Swaraj*. However, *Swaraj* is understood differently by different persons. Nripendra Chandra Banerjee rightly describes the multiverse perceptions about Swaraj : "(It is) the dream of a poetic mind, the mirage of a dry intellectual, the gossamer-thread of a philosopher, spinning his ideas, the incessant topic of street discussion, the bane and an athema to be the committee-harnessed school master, the apple of discord in debating clubs, the object of laughter in many of our bar-associations and the golden apple guarded by the sleepless eyes of non-cooperation.[20] It means so many things to so many persons—*absolute* unqualified independence, domination status, a system of political make-shifts, Dharma-rājya, world-federation etc. In the words of C.R. Das, "Swaraj is Vedantic freedom of soul in universe of free community of souls".[21]

In its evolution, the Vedic *Sva-rajya* has travelled a long distance upto the modern concept of *Swaraj*. For some time, especially during the pick period in our freedom-movement, Swaraj had become synonymous with political independence although Gandhi tried his best to emphasise the moral and spiritual dimension of it by writing his *Hind Swaraj* as early as in *1908* and continued reminding till the day of his martyrdom in his Last Testament. He tried to assimilate the spiritual content of the Vedas together with the moral element depicted in the concept of Ram-Rajya, and also infuse it with the socio-political and economic dynamism of the modern times.

Gandhi's Contribution to Swaraj : Square of Swaraj

Hence Gandhi's Swaraj is not one-dimensional, not utopian, not purely scholastic and yet it is refreshing, somewhat original and futuristic as well as realistic. As a practical idealist or like Wordsworth's skylark, he was true to both *Heaven* and *Earth*. He had his feet firmly footed on the Indian soil and for him Indian nationalism was not exclusive, nor aggressive, nor destructive.[22] He was wedded to India because, he said, "I owe my all to her".[23] He would not flinch from sacrificing even a million lives for India's liberty[24] and would like to bury himself in an Indian village, preferably in a frontier village.[25] Even with such intensely emotional attachment to India, Gandhi had a global vision. "Through the deliverance of India, I seek to deliver the socalled weaker races of the earth from the crushing heels of western exploitation".[26] Hence he openly declared, "The Indian struggle is not anti-British, it is anti-exploitation, anti-foreign-rule, not anti-foreigners".[27] On India rests the burden of pointing the way of all the exploited races of the earth. Hence while Gandhi cannot compromise with the right to govern oneself. He said passionately : We must be content to die, if we cannot live as free men and women".[28] As every country is fit to eat, to drink and to breathe, even so is every nation fit to manage its own affairs, no matter now badly".[29]

Hence mere withdrawal of the English was no independence for him, far less Swaraj. By Swaraj he meant "the government by the consent of the people as ascertained by the largest number of adult population. In other words",[30] his Swaraj was *by the people and for the people*. It was neither a theocratic order nor a rest house of the capitalistis. He said, "The Swaraj of my dream recognises no race or religious distinction. Nor it is to be the monopoly of the latter persons nor yet of monied men. Swaraj is to be for all, including the farmer, but emphatically including the maimed, the blind, the starving, toiling millions".[31] Hence Gandhi's political dimension of Swaraj has humanitarian, democratic and pro-poor angle. There is no narrow or aggressive nationalism. His notion of *Purna Swaraj* is not of isolated independence but healthy and dignified interdependence".[32] Political dimension of Sva-rajya (Swaraj) means that the people of the country must have complete control over all political institutions. For this, he was dead against the parliamentary system of representative democracy, because centralism is engrained in it and where there is centralisation of power, violence comes in. He wanted a national life as far self-regulated as possible. He would prefer a participatory democracy at the grass roots instead a centralised bureaucratic order. To him like Thoreau that government is best which governs the least. He looked "upon an increase in the power of the State with the greatest fear, because although while apparently doing good by minimizing exploitation, it does the greatest harm to mankind by destroying the individuality which lies at the root of all progress".[33] He was, however, non-compromising on the problem of adoption of violence for political or social change. He said, "Swaraj established by non-violent means will be different in kind from the Swaraj that can be established by armed rebellion".[34] Violent means will give violent Swaraj. That would be a menace to the world and India itself.[35] He was therefore convinced that "true democracy can only be outcome of non-violence".[36] Though he was an emancipator and a liberator, he was not in favour of isolated independence but for "voluntary inter-dependence".[37] He did not hate politics but he was always in favour of politics with principle. He therefore advocated purity of means and a 'goodness politics'.

(b) Economic Sva-rajya

Apparently, it looks that Gandhi was aloof from politics but he was away only from power-politics and party-politics. "Politics encircle us today like the coil of the snake from which one cannot get out, no matter how much one tries".[38] Therefore he was in politics, though his constructive programme was in no way less or subordinate to political work. But he felt rightly that to a certain extent his "social or constructive work would be impossible without the help of political work".[39]

But politics is also rooted in economics. Every human being has a right to live, and therefore to find the wherewithal to feed himself and where necessary, to clothe and house himself.[40] According to him "the economic constitution of India and for the matter of that of the world, should be such that no one under it should suffer for want of food and clothing".[41] But he did not favour giving alms or doles and instead advocated 'Gospel of work' or 'Bread Labour' described in the Gita as *yajna*. He tried to combine the secular and immediate needs with his philosophical approach to the entire development problem. He had a holistic conception of development-material, social, cultural and moral development. Hence, he wanted to create moral basis for Economic progress. To him, "true economics never militates against the highest ethical standard".[42] In Gandhi, man emerges at the centre of all economic or political development. Hence he challenged the technological basis of modern civilization, which has caused environmental pollution. Where population pressure is too high to sustain on the per capita land available, it should not displace human labour. Where heavy and large-scale industries are inevitable they should be under producer's control. All production should be for constumption and not for Profit. Production and Consumption should be localised. Gandhi defined basic needs in terms of material and non-material needs. He did not accept multiplication of wants as the yardstick of progress. Hence he did not regard the western living standard as its ideal. It was an hindrance to man's spiritual or higher aspiration. Hence he was against indiscriminate large-scale mechanisation of life. All these point out towards Gandhi's relevance to the present predicament.

(c) Social Dimension of Svarajya

Political or economics emerge out of social context. So he was always engaged in a social revolution. He wanted "to bring about an equalization of status".[43] He felt that the working classes have all these centuries been isolated and relegated to a lower status, called the *Shoodras*. Even social aparthied in the form of untouchability was practiced. Hence Gandhi started a crusade for the abolition of untouchability. He want further and advocated to bring at par both the brain-workers amid the manual workers, for both of them perform useful social work. He did not like to see a managerial class with vested interests to develop to create a division between the white coloured and the manual labourers. Hence, although he had admiration for the fourfold division of society based on profession and occupation, he admitted that now it is no more in practice. Hence, he thought that "the present case system is the very anti-thesis of Varnashrama. The sooner public opinion abolishes it is better".[44] Caste has nothing to do with religion. It is harmful both to spiritual and national growth. He was radical enough to declare castes as mere labels." To him, the question of food and drink has or ought to have no social value,[45] and there should be no prohibition of intermarriage or interdining.[46] He also fought for gender injustices like child marriages, the dowry system, compulsory widowhood, Purdah etc. He was "firmly of opinion that India's salvation depends on the sacrifice and enlightment of her women".[47] In his opinion, "It is degrading both for man and woman that woman should be called upon or induced to forsake the hearth and shoulder the rifle for the protection of that hearth".[48] He brought many enlightened women to the freedom struggle as well as to the constructive work. Gandhi's crusade against communalism is as well known as his herculian fight against racial discrimination in South Africa. Education and skill in some productive work will go a long way to equalise the status of women.

(d) Spiritual Dimension of Swarajya

The first step to Swaraj does not lie in political, economic or social systems but in the individual. Hence, Government over self is the trust Swaraj, it is synonymous with *Moksha* or salvation.[49] Swaraj of a people means the sum total of the Swaraj (Self-rule) of individuals.[50] Spiritual Swaraj, according to Gandhi, can be achieved only after the achievement of first three as it is based on the duties that each individual has to perform towards his society.

Swaraj depends entirely upon our own internal strength, upon our ability to fight against the heaviest odds. Political self-government is no better than individual self-government, and therefore, it is attained by precisely the same means that are required for individual self-government or self-rule.[51] Evolution is always experimental. All progress is gained through mistakes and their rectification. No good comes fully fashioned out of God's hand, but has to be carved out through our efforts and repeated experiments. Hence, "the attempt to win Swaraj is Swaraj itself".[52] Hence, purity of means was his greatest concern. As the means, so the end. Swaraj was not only a form of government or an economic order but it was "synonymous with *Ram Raj*—the establishment of the kingdom of Righteousness on earth".[53] But his love for Ram or Ram-Raj was ingrained in his selfless love for starving millions of India. Gandhi's spiritualism was never cut off from practical affairs. He said, "If any action of men claimed to be spiritual is proved to be unpractical it must be pronounced to be a failure. I do believe that the most spiritual act is the most practical in the true sense of the term".[54] Hence could not "conceive politics as divorced from religion". Here religion does not mean sectarianism. It means a belief in ordered moral government of the universe".[55] His views on Ethical Religion with his eleven moral vows are the basis of his moral and spiritual basis of *Swaraj.*

Conclusion

Gandhi's Swaraj is a philosophy of civilization and cultural liberation. Not stopping as a theoretical exposition of the concept, it comes with his commitment to its realisation and as a confession of faith. While political freedom was his immediate task but it is like an ice-berg. His concept of Swaraj started a debate on Indian Civilization and modern civilization. While *Swaraj* was the watchword of every Indian during the freedom struggle, all did not mean the same thing by it. To the Extremists, it meant only driving out the British but interested in British Parliamentary system, British trained army. Even the Moderates had great liking for the British polity. Perhaps this is the result that we have accepted England's parliamentary system and Govt. of India Act of 1935, as the basis of our Constitution, with some necessary Cosmetics. Almost all the values of freedom struggled were relegated to the Directive Principles of State Policy, which are non justiceable.

This was not the constitution of *Swaraj* that Gandhi wanted because it was not truly Swaraj. He was frank or even harsh in characterising British Parliamentary democracy as a prostitution or sell-out of freedom to party-political pressure by manufactured majority and even through corrupt and unfair practices. Parliament is a costly toy and a big talking shop.

Hence, instead of Swaraj, we have worse plight. But this has to be understood as a civilizational crisis. India is fast in the race of accepting the materialist culture of the west in the name of modernity. Religious and moral considerations have become either extraneous or are dismissed as superstitions. The virtue of self-control is being replaced by growing consumerism the sense of duty has been given a good bye and replaced by rights. Violence has grown and even Satyagraha has been replaced by *Duragrah*. Hence what is needed is not only "rethinking" or an "arm-chair gossip" but a certain amount of commitment for "emancipation". Gandhi says: "Only the fringe of the ocean has been polluted, it is those who are within the fringe alone need cleansing".[56]

REFERENCES

1. *Aitreya Brahman,* Eight kinds of polity are as follows : *Sāmrājyam, Bhaugyam, Svavayyam, Vairagyam, Parmesthyam Rajyam, Maharajyam, Adhipatyamayam and Samanta Paryayi.*

2. Rg Veda, V. 66.6.

3. Gandhi, M.K., *Hind Swaraj,* Ahmedabad : Navajiwan, 1st ed. 7th reprint, 1989, p. 55.

4. Gandhi, M.K., *Young India,* 8-1-1925.

5. *Bhagvadgita,* II. 47.

6. Quoted by Mahadeva Desai, The Gita According to

Gandhi, Ahmedabad, Navajiwan, 1st ed. 4th impression, 1956, p. 161.

7. Holy Quran, X.72.

8. *Ibid.*, XXI. 22.

9. Gandhi, M.K., *Young India*, 15-3-28.

10. Gandhi, M.K., Quoted by Tendulkar, *Mahatma*, New Delhi : Publications Division, 2nd ed. 1960, Vol. II. p. 300.

11. Toffler, Alvin, Power-Shift, (Paper back ed.) ISBN. 18052, From Personal Preface, p. XVIII.

12. *Ibid.*, p. 464.

13. Dhawan, G.N., "Goodness Politics", *Politics of Persuation*, ed. Mishra, K.P. and Avasthi, R., Bombay, Manaktalas, 1967, pp. 336-339.

14. Jaspers, K., "Gandhi and His 100th Birthday" *Mahatma Gandhi : 100 years*, ed. S. Radha Krishnan, New Delhi: Gandhi Peace Foundation, 1968, p. 170.

15. Kunzru, H.N., "Spiritualise Politics", *Mahatma Gandhi: 100 Years, op. cit.*, p. 224.

16. *Rg Veda*, III.30.6; Atharva Veda, XV. 2.9.2; XIX. 7.55.6.

17. *Satpath Brahman*, XIII, 2.3.

18. *Rv Veda*, I.39.2.

19. *Rajdharman Pravakshyami, Manu-Smrti, Mahabhaṭu etc.*

20. Banerji, N.P., *The Ideal of Swaraj*, Madras : Ganesh and Co., 1921, p. 47.

21. *Ibid.*, p. 48.

22. Tendulkar, D.G., *Mahatma*, II.p. 64.

23. *Ibid.*, II. p. 6.

24. *Ibid.*, III. 152.

25. *Ibid.*, III. 299.

26. *Ibid.*, Mind of the Mahatma, ed. Prabhu & Rao, 3rd ed. 1968, p. 315.

27. Tendulkar, D.G., *Ibid.*, V. p. 255.

28. Gandhi, M.K., *Young India*, 5.1.22.

29. *Ibid.*, 15.10.31.

30. *Ibid.*, 29.1.25.

31. *Ibid.*, 3.9.25.

32. *Ibid.*, 26.3.31.

33. Gandhi, M.K., *Young India*, 2.3.22.

34. Gandhi, M.K., Modern Review, Oct. 1935, p. 412.

35. *Ibid.*, Y.I., 17.7.24.

36. Gandhiji's Correspondence with the Govt., 1942-44, Madras, 1930, p. 175.

37. Gandhi, M.K., *Young India*, 17.7.24.

38. Gandhi, M.K., *Young India*, 12.5.20.

39. *Ibid.*, *Young India*, 6.8.31.

40. *Speeches and Writings of M. Gandhi*, ed. G.A. Natesan, Madras, p. 350.

41. Gandhi, M.K., *Young India*, 15.11.28.

42. Gandhi, M.K., *Harijan*, 9.10.37.

43. Gandhi, M.K., *Harijan*, 15.1.38.

44. Gandhi, M.K., *Harijan*, 16.11.35.

45. *Ibid.*, *Young India*, 29.12.20.

46. *Ibid.*, *Harijan*, 16.11.35.

47. *Ibid., Harijan,* 27.6.36.

48. *Ibid., Harijan,* 24.4.40.

49. *Ibid., Harijan,* 8.12.20.

50. *Ibid., Harijan,* 25.3.39.

51. Desai, M., *With Gandhiji in Ceylon,* Ganeshan, S., Madras, 1928, p. 93.

52. *Speeches and Writings of Mahatma Gandhi,* Madras, Natesan, 4th ed., p. 685.

53. *Young India.,* 4.5.21.

54. *Harijan,* 1.7.39.

55. *Harijan,* 10.2.40.

56. Gandhi, Hind Swaraj (*Chhutkara*), p. 93.

Chapter 12

SARVODAYA AS ECO-SPIRITUALITY

Contrary to the view that there is an inherent conflict between Man and Nature, the *Bhumi Suktam* of *Atharva Veda,*[1] speaks of the Earth as the sustained of the human race, and the necessity to nourish and protect the earth from despoilation. That human being as the children of God, as the finest and the best in God's creation hold the key, through contentment and self-abnegation (is sharp contrast to acquisition through avarice and greed) to the sustenance of the universe has been forcefully brought out in these words of the Isavasyopnisad[2] :

> Please remember that this world is the Lord's creation
> And everything that exists here in His
> He pervades the whole universe
> Be content with whatever is lift by Him
> And do not greed the wealth of others.

The control of nature is a phrase concieved in arrogance born of the Neanderthal age of "Biology and Philosophy" when it was supposed that nature exists for the convenience of man".[3]

Even Mediaval Christianity also held that physical creation had any purpose except to serve man's purpose. Therefore Lyn White Jr. has said that "especially in the western form, Christianity is the most anthropocentric religion the world has seen" and "Christianity bears a huge burden of guilt" for environmental Crises.[4] But an alternative Christian view of the human-non-human relationship is well reflected in the life of St. Francis of Assisi who attempted "to depose man from his monarchy over creation and set up a democracy of all God's creatures".[5] For the Israelite, nature is something that is to be sub-ordinated to man. In the book of genesis we road as follows : "Let us make man is our own image and likeness; and let them have dominion over the fish of the sea, and over the birds of the air, and over the cattle, and over all the earth and over every creeping thing that creeps upon the earth."......(1/26). Again, "Be fruitful and multiply and fill the earth and subdue it; and have dominion over the fish of the sea." (1/28). Interestingly this Judo-Christian view of divine sanction of domination, led even the scientists. Like Francis Bacon proclaim that the "Conquest of nature" was the goal of science. However, we cannot deny there is a profound and deepening of the importance of our treatment of one another and especially the weak and oppressed. (St. Mathew, 25/40) Godi care for the "grass of the field and the fallen sparrow", these too are evidences of the non-exploitation nature of animals and vegetable kingdom by man. Hence, "the anthropocentric ethic, understood as an emphasis on human well-being at the expense of the earth and other living beings, must the replaced by an ethic of respect for life and environment".[6]

The Indian way of life embraces all aspects of the life and their interrelationships. We can point out the two underlying principles—(1) Sanctity of life and (2) the unity of man and nature. Yajur Veda says : Universe comes to have one home; therein unites and therefore emanates the whole, the Omnipresent One pervades souls and matter like the warp and woof in created beings".[7] The principle of sanctity of life flows from the idea of the Divine Being as the one underlying power of unity. The sacredness of God's creation means no damage may be inflicted on other species without adequate justification. Therefore all lives, human and non-human, are of equal value and all have the same right to existence. The principle of sanctity of life," is permeated by a 'reverence for life'.[8] Incidentally Schwitzer also advocates 'reverence for life' or the non-violence. Another ecological dimension is the conception of the "unity of man and nature". Nature was not a sum of objects to be used or manipulated. Nature or Prakriti was the very sources of life. Atharveda says : "The Earth is the Mother, I am son of Earth. The rain-gives is my father, may be shown on us blessings".[9]

Hence, the ecological crisis is essentially a religious and philosophical crisis. It is a question of survival not only of human life but all forms of life, may even the material world. God pervades everywhere and in every particle of matters. Hence, we have to develop a cosocentric perspective. Hence to Gandhi, "God manifests Himself in innumerable forms in the universe and every such manifestation commands my spontaneous reverence".[10]

He wanted to understand nature as an expression of God and tried to see life in everything breaking down even the customary distinction between the animate and the inanimate. He drew inspiration from the modern sacrifice researches. The idea of the continuity through different forms of being got confirmation even from Darwinian theory of evolution. But the Darwinion theory was taken by Gandhi as supporting the idea of gradual progress. Gandhi's call for "Return to Nature", his fondness for naturopathy was an indication of this temper. Man has to learn to live in harmony nor only with his fellows beings but with the entire nature - animate as well as inanimate. That we should live together in peace is the basic ethics of all ethics.

Eco-Ethics is an inseparable part of Eco-Theology and Eco-Philosophy. During the Vedic period, they observed *Agnihotra* (oblation to the fire) for cleansing the pollution of the environment. Oblations offered goes in the clouds blotting near the earth, bringing rain Materials being offered in the sacrificial fire are more or less hydroscopic in nature.

If modern science brought man standing against Nature and God, Eco-philosophy brings him back to Nature and Godess that man no longer poses himself as the conqueror of nature but experience himself/herself as continuation and fulfilment of both nature and cosmos. For the ancient Greeks it was the principle of Harmony between Man and Nature, with Christianity it was Redemptions, for the Modern Man of Enlightment and science, it was Freedom and Reason. It is the principle of wholeness, of Oneness, Non-duality there man is again reconnected in the inter-connection of the man-history-cosmos-continuum. We are living is in world divided politically, economically and racially. There are only a few rich nations. For example U.S.A. with a population of 6% of the consumes about 40% of world resources. The affluent nations within their specialized knowledge plunder the planet in the name of development. Cursed with poverty and illiteracy, the poor nations are constrained to use Nature for their need. Hence they connect afford to conserve Nature when the rich nations are living a life of affluence. Unless the humanity has to perceive the prime need to develop on the principle of "One Earth" and "One World" with a spirit of sharing and just distribution of Nature's wealth cutting across the nationalistic boarders, we cannot achieve a sustainable development. Living with a sense division, separation and discrimination is detrimental to a healthy and meaningful life and peaceful world.

Here the prescription of Sarvodaya is most relevant for it treats the whole world as a family—*Vasudhaiv Kutumbkam.* It does not believe in narrow nationalism or chauvinism. Gandhi said : "Nationalism is not the highest concept. The highest concept is world community. I would not like to live in this world if it is not to be one world." Sri Aurbindo endorsed this view in his the ideal of Human Progress : "The creation of a World State is the logical and inevitable outcome. Narrow nationalism and religious sectarianism have brought immense miseries to the world. They have made the world worse. The nation-states and the personal religions have created not only territorial discrimination but also divided mankind. Hence, a world Govt. based on maximum individual freedom and a world economy based on economic justice and the principle of sustainable development are imperatives of this age. Gandhi therefore said that his nation of Purana Swaraj is not isolated independence but healthy and dignified interdependence. "My nationalism, fierce though it is, is not exclusive, not designed to harm any nation or individual".[12] "Through Swaraj we would serve the whole world".[13] He further says : "I would like to all India free and strong so that she may after herself as a willing and pure sacrifice for the betterment of the world".[14] Thus Gandhi's "nationalism was not inconsistent with progressive internationalism".[15] A man whose spirit of sacrifice did not go beyond his own community became selfish himself and also made his community selfish. A truly independence India was bound to run to help of its neighbours in distress.[16]

Gandhi knew that the cause of the present chaos is exploitation not only of the weaker nations by the stronger, but of sister nations by sister nations. Economic equality is the master key to non-violent independence. At the root of equal distribution live the Gandhian principle of trusteeship. The wealth of the world is a common property. We are only its trustees. Hence, coal or mica of India or wheat grown in U.S.A. should be treated as common property of the world. India suffers from over-population where as Australia needs population. In short, if we can evolve an world economic order based on justice and need of the whole of humanity, there is less scope for strife. Nature produces enough for our wants but if we indulge in cruel exploitation of nature, we will face many problems including environmental disasters.

So the root cause of ecological imbalances and disasterless in our extravagant style of life. No doubt, nature produces enough for our wants but there is limitation to it. There is no limit to our desires. Excessive consumption or rather extravagance has been half-mark of our civilization. There should be self-restraint exercised in every sphere of life. If we go on increasing our wants, we shall need such instruments which can exploit natural resources more and more. Hence our unbriddled desires for more and more comforts and luxuries implies that we should have a particular model of development and for that model of development, we need a particular technology. The modern Sensate civilization, is the root cause of environmental problems. Hence, like Socrates and Gandhi, Rifken, the author of *Entropy* pleaded for a simpler life-style in the name of Second Law of Thermodynamics. Gandhi has rightly said that "Nature has given enough to satisfy our needs but not our greed". He goes further to assert that "the world does not have sufficient things to meet the greed of a single person".[17] Hence we need a new design of living Arnold Toynbee has shown that rare and luxury had been the most vital foes of the 27 civilizations which have pursued into oblivion of antiquity. The mind is like a restless bird, the more gets, the more it wants and still remains unsatisfied.

The rich are discontented no less than the poor. The poor man would gain a millionaire, and the millionaire a multi-millionaire.[18]

Material gain has not necessarily meant moral gain. Rome suffered a moral fall when it attained high material affluence. So did Egypt and so perhaps most countries of which we have any historical record.[19] These might be many remedies to chick pollution like treatment of factories etc. but unless we have treatment of our extra vagancies, we shall be constrained to exploit nature most mercilessly and unscrupulously leading to holes in the ozone layers and nuclear winter etc. The indiscriminate technology has turned man into exploiter with utmost selfishness, envoy and violence.

Conclusion

Gandhi and Sarvodaya have been branded as anti-science and anti-progressively because one does not appreciate the value of Gandhi's philosophy of *wants* and *needs,* which were conditioned by self-control and limitation. He was not in favour of unlimited multiplication of wants and needs. Hence the concept of the so-called standard of living, which the west has been able to achieve was not acceptable to Gandhi because of two reasons— *(a)* First it was an obstruction to man's, spiritual and higher aspirations, and *(b)* Secondly, given the present historical context, such as standard of living was unrealisable within a short time. It might take 100 to 150 years and there is no end to it. Hence his whole philosophy of development and progress and civilization was replaced. The industrial revolution gave birth to wrong and civilization. We were dazzled by the light of machines and gadgets but we lost our balance. Modern civilization has taught us to convert night into day and golden silence into brazen din and noise. Air, water, the two boons of nature to all living being and the basis of our life have been polluted and have posed serious threat to life. During winter in Berlin, children suffer from pseudocrap due to concentration of polluted air in certain places. According to Russian scientists, the oxygen requirements of technosphere are fifteen times more than those of living beings. The forests of U.S.A., Canada and Europe have become the victims of acid ruins. Growing tendency to exploit energy with the problem of disposal of the waste is a major anxiety. The so-called modern technology is linked up not only with modern economic political ideology but also with war, which eats up more than 600 billions dollars per year. According to Fritzof Capra, "nuclear power is neither safe, nor clean, nor cheap. The 360 nuclear reactors now operating word-wide, and the hundreds more planned, have become a major threat to our well-being... with their continuing proliferation, the likelihood of global extinction becomes greater everyday".[20] Studies show that today American contain 500 times more lead than those of prehistoric humans.[21]

When fossils fuels are burnt, sulphur-dioxides of nitrogen are released into the air. This acid rain is most dangerous for human life.[22] So ozon depletion would cause serious harm to humans, after mammals, plants, birds, insects and some sea-life.[23] A study by the U.S. Environmental Protection Agency in 1970s found that water suppliers of 80% American cities contained chemicals that may cause Cancer.[24] The U.S. Global 2000 Report says that the demand for fresh water in the world will increase by 200 to 300% from 1975 to 2000 A.D.[25] Cleaning of toxic waste has cost U.S. 1.6 billion dollars but the Congressional office of Technological Assessment has estimated that it will require about 50 year and 100 billion dollars to clean.[26] Due to pesticides and insecticides, one million species are bound to be extinct.

Environmental hazards of the modern times have not only threatened our physical and biological existence but also has caused intellectual and moral degradation. In a suffocating and highly contaminated atmosphere, much of our creativity, freedom and initiative is lost. There is always a fear of insecurity, depression and frustration which has been described by Alvin Toffler in his book Future Shock.[27]

The environmental problem has given a rude shock to the blind march towards this industrial culture. We have to develop a Man—Man and Man-Nature relation. What is necessary is not a high standard of living but a richer quality of life. What is required is a life natural—an ecological balance between man, animals, vegetables and material-mineral-hydraulic world. If the world is becoming a global village, it must also have a global ethics. Similarly, environmental education is a must both at the formal and non-formal level. Environment ethics came be compared by law. Hence environmental education is very important factor to bring it to the doorsteps of each and every individual. The club of Rome thesis on the *Limits to Growth* or the Stockholm Conference in 1972 proclaiming the protection of the environment, Rio's Earth Summit in 1992 and Social Summit at Copenhegan in 1997 and numerous Reports and Resolutions only confirm the Sarvodaya philosophy of Life and Living. The real enemy of environment lies written our own mental frame—our unbriddled desires and wants. We cannot be both rolling in luxuries as well as guarantee safety of our mother earth. Voluntary limitation of our wants through self-control is the panecea.

REFERENCES

1. *Atharva Veda,* Prithvi Mahamena Sukta.

2. *Isa Upanishad.*

3. Fox, Warvik, *Towards a Transpersonal Ecology,* 1990, p. 5.

4. White, Lyn. Jr., "The Historical Roots of our Ecological Crises", *Science,* March, 10, 1967. Vol 155, No. 3767.

5. *Ibid.,* p. 1206.

6. Birch, Charles, (ed.), *Liberating Life,* Orbis Books, 1991, p. 1.

7. *Yajur Veda,* 32.8.

8. Engel, D., and Engel, J.G., (ed.) *Ethics of Environment and Development,* Bethaven, 1990, p. 53.

9. *Atharva Veda, (Prithvi Sukta).*

10. Gandhi, *Young India,* 26.3.29.

11. Just's *Retrun to Nature.*

12. Gandhi, M.K., *Young India,* 26.3.31.

13. *Ibid.,* 16.4.31.

14. *Ibid.,* 17.9.25.

15. Amrit Bazar Patrika, Calcutta, 17.9.33.

16. Gandhi, M.K., *Harijan,* 23.3.47.

17. Fernandes, Angelo., "God's Rule and Mans Role", *Gandhi Marg,* March 1982, p. 699.

18. Gandhi, M.K., *From Yervada Mandir,* Ahmedabad, Navajivan, 1935, p. 311.

19. *Ibid., Speeches and Writings of M. Gandhi,* Madras, G.A. Nalisan, 4th ed., p. 350.

20. Fritzof Capra, *The Turning Point, Science, Society and the Rising Culture,* London, 1983.

21. *New York Times,* 13.5.1982.

22. Commoner, L.B., *The Closing Circle,* New York Alfred Knopf, 1971, p. 39.

23. Eckholm, E., *Down To Earth,* New York, W.W. Morton, 1982, p. 95.

24. Stoler, Peter, "Is clean water a thing of the Past?

25. *The Global 2000 Report to the President,* New York, Penguin Book, 1982, p. 26.

26. Levine, Adiline., *Lone Lonal, Science, Politics and People,* Levington, 1982, Michael Brown, Laying Waste, The Poisoning of Amercia by Toxic Wesle, New York, Pantheon Books, 1980, New York Times.

27. Tofler Alvin, Future Shock, New York, 1911.

Chapter 13

UNIVERSAL MAN AND UNIVERSAL RELIGION

The test of every religious, political or educational system is the man that it forms. Alexander Pope rightly says : "The proper study of mankind is man". But what is man? —"Half dust, half dirty, alike unfit to sink or soar"— Byron. Somebody sings his glory, somebody else treats him as beasts. Shakespeare exclaims—"What a piece of work is man! How noble is reason! How infinite in faculties! In form and moving how express and admirable! In action, how like an angel! In apprehension, how like a god!" This is why, he is regarded as the crowning wonder of creation. But then there are others who depict man as beasts—"a frowning dog, a roaring lion, a thriving fox, a robbing wolf, a dissembling crocodile, a treacherous decoy, and a rapacious vulture." English poet Abhram Cowley. It seems that perhaps he is both. Hence it is dangerous to represent man as to how near he is to the level of beasts, without showing him at the same time his greatness. Similarly, it is dangerous to let him see his greatness. Without his meanness. "It is more dangerous yet to leave him ignorant of either; but very beneficial that he should be made sensible of both"— says Pascal.

None of the above views about man may be adequate because all of them try to understand human nature from a superficial standpoint, based on external behaviour. All of them emphasise upon the physical and material aspect of man.

Indian philosophy tries to harmonize the psychologists and the metaphysicians because it is the search after unity. It also does not care for the particular; it is always after the general, nay universal. But this universal cosmic entity splits into the soul of man. Though evil and good are both conditioned manifestations of the soul, yet evil is the most external coating, and good is the nearer coating of the real man, the Self. Unless a man cuts through the layer of evil, he cannot reach the layer of good, and unless the possesses through both the layers of good and evil, he cannot reach the Self. It is the universal cosmic mind that splits into many things and beyond mind we have found in soul in us. In the universe, behind the universal mind, there is the Soul that exists. In short, there is real and the apparent man—one all-comprehending existence, and that appears as manifold. This Self, or Soul, or Substance, is all that exists in the universe, which appears as manifold by the interposition of name and form. It is like the sea and its waves. Not one wave is really different from the sea, but what makes the waves apparently different? Name and form, the form of the wave, and the name which we give to it, 'wave'. That is what makes it different from the sea. Not one wave is really different from the sea. When name and form go, it is the same sea. So this whole universe is that One Unit Existence, name and from have created all these various differences. But it is in reality only one. There is no 'I' nor 'you', it is all One. It is neither all 'I' or all 'you'. The idea of duality is entirely false. There is therefore one *Self,* eternally perfect, unchangeable, unchanged. Various changes in the universe are but appearances in that one Self. Each man consists of three parts—the body, the internal organ or the mind, and behind that, what is called Self (*Atman*). The body is the external coating, and the mind is the internal coating of the Atman who is the real perceiver, the real enjoyer, the being in the body by means of the internal organ of the body or the mind. The Self is the only existence in the human body which is immaterial, and since it is immaterial it is not a compound and because it is not compound, it does not obey the law of cause and effect, and so we can call it immortal, which has no beginning and hence no end. It must be also formless for there cannot be any form without matter. Our body will perish as it has a beginning but the Self having no form cannot be bound by the law of beginning and end. It is in existence from infinite time; just as time is eternal, so is the Self of man, eternal. Secondly it must be all-pervading because that which is formless cannot be confined in space. So the Self is in me, in you, in everyone and therefore omnipresent. It never comes or goes, is never born nor dies. It neither moves. Darwinism looms large on our mind when it says that man evolves out of animal. If we have a soul so they should have, and if they have none, neither have we. It is absurd to say that man alone has a soul, and the animals noye. There are men worse than animals.

Modern man is in search of Soul, says Jung. The scripture says—"I exist in all beings as the Self". So "Know thyself" is the key word of the Upanisads as well as of Socrates. One who sees the entire universe in his Self and Self in the entire universe, there is no cause of any worry and anxiety for him.[1] But how can we understand this spiritual nature of man, if we treat him as the Economic Man (Adam Smith) of "Sexual creature" (Freud) or as an animal engaged in the "struggle for existence" (Darwin)? Man is not all physical and psychological but essentially divine and spiritual. Hence logically he inherits the qualities of God, who is said to be possessor of all excellences. Hence man's goodness follows from the goodness of God.

But then how can we explain the presence of evil impulses in man? This is because man is not perfect being like God. He is not pure soul but a combination of body and soul. Hence he has emotions, passions and impulses also as they are necessary resultant of our physical frame. But they can be reformed. Hence there is the evolutionary progress of man. History is the saga of man's striving to discover his humanity, which is but a reflection of the Supreme. God is perfect hence man's goal is perfection. Man's nature is not essentially evil because he is definitely going higher everyday. Even fallen and thoroughly debased man is capable of rising to the greatest height. Hence we find that in the midst of death, life persists, in the midst of hatred, love persists.

One can say that to regard human nature as basically good, we indulge in false generalisation based on bad psychology. But supposing this is wrong and the critics are right and that man is by nature evil, then the result would be to draw a very dismal picture of life. All efforts at purification and reformation will go in vain. To consider man or woman as naturally evil is not only an insult to the whole human race, it is also a counsel of despair. True, we find anger, lust, envy in man but this is not his essential nature. They are due to his attachment to this body. Soul is pure, free and absolutely unattached with evil. He can free himself from evil through moral and spiritual discipline. This explains his potential divinity.

Another criticism against such a view about Self is that it obliterates the distinction between the *ideal* and the *actual*. From the position "man ought to be good" one derives the conclusion that "man is actually good". But this is not so. Nobody denies the presence of good and evil in man. Everyone of us is a combination of both good evil. Spiritually he is pure and good but while he is in the body, he is tied down by the shackles of flesh. He is no doubt imperfect but he always endeavours to be perfect. In short, he is a harmonious combination of gross animal body, intellect and heart of the soul. Out side universe is the reflection of the inside universe. The universe is universe compressed in the atoms. There is not one law for the atoms and another for the universe.

The concept of human nature and its progress is in conformity with the sociological findings. The human civilization has been a march from barbarity to civilization from egoistic struggle to altruistic existence. Mankind has steadily progressed towards love and it is bound to progress further. Perhaps we were cannibals in the beginning but many of us would not like to kill a beast or even hurt a fly. Vegetarianism as a food habit and pacifism as a social-political cult is growing popular.

But apart from his spirituality, man's sociality is also established. True, his physical body is personal and individual, his mind and heart is social and universal. Leave aside Aristotle's thesis that "man is a social animal", the entire findings of modern science go to upholkd this view. The perenial adventures in civilization are threefold :

(1) To bring forth the integrated and complete kind of man—the Universal Man that has emerged in all epochs of human history.

(2) To find out and achieve the intrinsic, ultimate and transcendent values that are more or less of perennial nature.

(3) To establish a society or communion that passes towards the unlimited continuity which is the cosmos.

Civilization in spite of its manifoldness is fundamentally one. Each major culture spells out its own notion of the complete and Universal Person, its intrinsic and instrumental values of life and the wholeness and harmony with the cosmos, corresponding to its spirit and genius, the accumulated force of myth, value and environment. It is false one sided western philosophy of history coming from Hegel and Marx that regards human cultures as more or less discrete and successive stages of phases in a unilinear, historical series. In fact cultures have parallel evolution, historically and logically contributing with its universally and rationally human elements towards and encircling the common heritage of mankind.

There is a tendency in civilizational dynamics of mankind to transcend time and changes in men and the flux of events into open pattern of persons-values and cosmos. Hence, the key-notions of civilization are the unity and wholeness. The conception of *Universal Man* alongwith universal values and universal community is the transcending principle of knowledge of civilization grasped only as super-historical reality. Universal Person in one's Neighbour. Every social relationship is the vehicle of Transcendence and every people, group of institution is an echo of cosmic community.

The three entities—Universal Person, Transcendent Values and Cosmic Community are facts of the same dynamic of civilization. The twentieth century is perhaps the sickest, most wicked, and bloodiest in human annals, possesses the highest potentials for a complete transformation and fulfilment of man and civilization, With the possibilities of the emergence Universal Man, Today the instruments and techniques of human degradation, mutilation and savegery thrive side by side with the great possibilities of the whole and Universal

Man and Cosmic Community. Knowledge, art, religion and morality combine in envisioning a metaphysical metacultural cosmic pattern of harmony, beauty and wholeness based on an ontological order encompassing man which alone can build up the unity and integrity of One World, One Civilization, One Noetic System, which can achieve the harmonious concord between man and society and civilization as a whole, and between man and the cosmos-total.[2]

The Universal Man is grounded in trans-humanism as neither Ethical Humanism from Comte to Russell confined mainly to the intellectual dimension nor Naturolistic-Humanism from Marx to Freud which has become an anthropocentric, myopic and sterile creed, but when man reaches his highest when he thinks, feels and lives beyond humanity when infinitude and eternity exist in his spiritual dialectic. The Universal Man is finite and yet bound by the Infinite.[3]

If we think of a Universal Man, we cannot think of a sectarian religion. Religion is the highest plane of thought and life but unfortunately on the one hand we find the intensest love that humanity has ever known, on the other hand the most diabolical hatred that humanity has witnessed. No other human motive has deluged the world with blood so much as religion. It is said that about 86% of wars and bloodshed have been caused in the name of religion. The crux of the problem even at the end of this millennium is how to being harmony among the religions.

Firstly, we have taken up religion as a mere play upon words and not a thing to be carried into practice (The Universal Religion, on p. 8 Middle Sex.1993). It becomes more or less like personal property as "my father's religion" or "nation's religion". In short, it becomes like a political phenomenon, a phase of narrow and sectarian patriotism. Hence as one ruler fights with the other, one religion does the same. Like Julius Caeser or Alexander, the religious leader wants to have world empire. At least, Christianity, Islam and Buddhism started with world-conquests, either through preaching, service, fraud or force. Jainism, Zorastrianism Judaism and Hinduism perhaps did not believe in prostylisation. The root cause of this religious imperialism is that "one's own religion is the most ancient, most universal and most useful for the mankind." Hence these, who think themselves as superior, think as their divine right to not only to propagate but to convert others into their fold through wilful or manipulated and forced conversion. We forget that religions are different roads converging to the same point. What does it matter if we take different roads. Hence, to think that one's own religion is the only way is undivine act. God has created different faiths just as He has the votaries thereof. Hence Gandhi asks: "How can I even secretly harbour the thought that my neighbour's faith is inferior to mine and wish that he should give up his faith and embrace mine?"[4] As a true and loyal friend, I can only wish and pray that he may live and grow perfect in his own faith. In God's house there are many mansions and they are equally holy.[5] Therefore Gandhiji with all good intentions advised the Christian Missionaries: "Your work will be all the richer if you accept as settled fact the faiths of the people you come to serve—faiths however crude, are valuable to them. I want you to complement the faith of the people instead of undermining it".[6] Hence a non-absolutistic attitude is necessary. To think that my religion is the best and the rest are in the clutches of devils and hence our sacred duty is to "civilize" them is a sacrilegious act. Hence, the institutions of conversion look like regiments of an army marching for aggression and carving out an empire. This has caused innumerable strikes, crusades, inquisitions and bloodshed in the world.

Religion is a very sacred and perennial affair. It is highly moral and spiritual phenomenon. No action which is not voluntary can be called a moral or spiritual and as soon as we loose that moral basis, we cease to be religious. All faiths constitute a revelation of Truth, but all are imperfect and liable to error. Besides, we cannot have the full vision of Truth, hence to think that our own faith is the best and the rest are inferior is again an indication of imperialism in thought. Hence the best way is to develop sincere reverence for all other faiths. There may be faults in them but we should be keenly alive to the defects of our own faith also and try to overcome them. We should also try to blend into our faith every acceptable feature of other faiths. "True knowledge of religion breaks down the barriers between faith and faith".[7] Study and appreciation of other religions need not cause a weakening of the religions rather it should mean extension of that regard to other religions. Hence, it is better to allow our lives to speak for us than words, than indulge in organised preaching. Speaking to Christian friends, Gandhi said : "Your work will be all the richer if you accept as settled fact the faiths of the people you come to serve—faith however crude, are valuable to them".[8] The time had passed when the followers of one religion could "stand and say, ours is the only true religion and all others are false." Hence co-existence and tolerance should be our guiding principle. He had chided Christian missionaries for their "irreligious gamble" for converts,[9] and in South Africa he exhorted the Arya Samaj against undertaking any missionary activity in that country. He did not permit proselyting in his ashrams.[10] Contrary to it, he did convert Miss Slade to Hinduism and asked her that she would find everything good in the Bible which she found in Hinduism. Richard Greg, who wrote extensively on non-violence and stayed in Gandhi's Ashram was called Govind but never became a Hindu. Gandhi's "religion is not a religion of the prison-house".[11] He did not "believe in the exclusive divinity of the Vedas. I believe the Bible, the Koran, and the Zend Avesta to be as much divinely inspired as the Vedas".[12] Religion to be religion of man should not be an exclusive. Gandhi "would not only not try to convert but would not even secretly pray that anyone should embrace my (his) faith".[13] Religion is a deeply personal matter, it touches the heart. Why should one change his religion because a doctor who professes some other religion has cured him to some disease. He did not believe that there is no such thing as conversion from one faith to another in the accepted term. It is highly personal matter for the individual and his God. "One should not have any design upon his neighbour as to his faith which one must honour as his own".[14] All prophets are equal. It is a horizontal plain. If we think in terms of Einstein's Relativity all are equal. But it is difficult to express that equality. That is why one should say that they are equally true and equally imperfect. One should not gloat over it any say mine is the superior one. "None is inferior to the other".[15] Fancis Young Husband confronted the question "Are all mothers equally good? All mothers are not equally good, but each would think his own mother as the best in the world".[16] But if we believe in the fundamental unity among all religions, this can be solved. Even if we regard our mother as best, it does not expect others to give up their own mothers and adopt ones own. Just as one's own mother is best for oneself, so is everyone's religion best, each for himself.[16] To create fellowship of faiths, it is not only to treat all religions as true, indulge into the study of comparative religion but also "Fellowship in Prayer".[17]

Universal Religion : Some Difficulties and Solutions

True the days of personal religion are over but religion is always and intensely a personal affair. But we can solve this paradox on the parlance of universal Man. Just as all individuals differ in colour, size, intelligence, power etc. but there is "an abstract humanity which is common to all", so it is with universal religion, which runs through all the various religions of the world in the form of God. God says : "I am the thread that runs through all these pearls" and each pearl is a religion or even a sect thereof.[18] Unity in diversity is the plan of the universe. The unity of sameness can come only when this universe is destroyed, otherwise such thing is impossible. Not only so, it would be dangerous to have it. We must not wish that all of us should think alike. It is this difference which is the soul of our progress, the soul of our thought.

So by a Universal Religion, we should not mean one Universal Philosophy or one mythology or any one universal ritual held alike by all. We have to recognise variation. We must learn that truth may be expressed in a manifold ways and each of these ways is ture as far as it goes. The same *Spirit* is everywhere and this is recognition of *universality*. Apart from this theoretical approach at working out harmony in religions, there are also practical ways. Firstly, we must have any plan which does not destroy the individuality of any man in religion and at the same time shows him a point of union with all others. Iconoclastic reformers do not good to the world. Then the second paradox is that in order to create religious harmony, it has been tried to bind them all down to a few doctrines, and so have produced more new sects, fighting, struggling and pushing against each other.[19] This is again adding one more religion in the list of numerous religions that we have "Universal Religion', therefore is not a new religion destroying or rejecting the existing religions. All existing religions are different forces in the economy of God working for the good of mankind : and that not one can become dead, not one can be killed. Just as we cannot kill any force in nature, so we cannot kill any one of these spiritual forces. As the universal brotherhood of man is already existing, so also is universal religion. There should be no worry to find greater number of sects, because then there is the more chance of people getting religion just like in a hotel where there are all sorts of food, everyone has a chance to get his appetite satisfied. That all these old religions are living today proves that they must have kept that missions insact, inspite of their mistakes and defects. They have not lost the great mission they came for. Islam has a great mission of brotherhood; with the Hindus they have the one national idea-spirituality; with the Christians, the central idea is purity and service. Hence "our watchword will be acceptance, and not exclusion".[20] Hence by universal Religion, we should not think of a separate or independent religion envisaged by Akbar the great in the name of Din-elahi. It is artificial. What is needed is to plead for the unity and equality of religions. Apart from the basic scriptures, the saints, seers and sufis etc. have strongly pleaded for the unity of man and unity of religions. Ram Krishna Paramhansa, the scriptural teacher of Swami Vivekanand had discovered an original dynamics of unity of religions. He did not only preach but shared in his own life the spiritual experiences of Islam, Christianity and Hinduism. I think this is by far the most exalted spiritual method of realizing Universal Religion. Tagore too advocated the "Religion of Man" rather than "religion of sect or community".

In fact, the days of "sectarian religion" and power-politics" are over. What is needed is a synthesis of Science and Spirituality. "Science is lame without religion, and religion is blind without science"—said Einstein. There are two kinds of reality or existence—the existence of our consciousness and the reality or existence of everything else. Cyril Hinshelwood therefore says: "To deny the reality of the inner world is a flat negation of all that is immediate in existence, to minimise its significance is to depreciate the very purpose of living, and to explain it away as a product of natural selection is a plain fallacy." Faith in the pursuit and value of science goes beyond science and reason. It is akin to a religious feeling : it goes beyond science. Faith in science, faith in reason is not anti-reason but beyond reason.[21] If science is universal, religion is also bound to be so, otherwise it is to be brushed aside as subjective. The climax of the ordinary consciousness is Science. For the religious consciousness, this empirical world is not the final reality. Laws are for the mind's convenience but the process of supramental manifestation is different. This is through yogic experience. Yoga is not subjective and personal it is as universal as science.

REFERENCES

1. *Isa Upanisad,* verses 6 & 7, *Bhagavadgita,* 6.32, 6.30.
2. Mukherjee, R.K., *The Universal Principles of Forms Civilizations,* Calcutta, R.K. Mission, 1961, p. 9.
3. Tagore, R.N., *Geetanjali,* London, Macmillan &1949, verse 1.
4. Gandhi, M.K., *Harijan,* 20-4-1934.
5. *Ibid., Harijan,* 20-4-1934.
6. *Ibid., Young India,* 11-8-27.
7. *Ibid., From Yervada Mandir,* 55.
8. *Ibid.,* 11-8-27.
9. *Ibid.,* p. 13.
10. *Ibid.,* p. 13.
11. *Ibid., Young India,* 1-6-1923.
12. *Ibid., Young India,* 6-1-1921.

13. *Ibid., Young India,* 19-1-28.

14. *Ibid., Harijan,* 28-1-1935.

15. *Ibid., Harijan,* 13-3-37.

16. Gandhi, M.K., *Fellowship of Faiths and Unity of Religions,* Delhi, Gandhi Book House, p. 38.

17. Vivekanand, *Fellowship in Prayer,* New Jersey, 1990, p. 2.

18. *Universal Religion,* New Jersy, p. 13.

19. *Ibid.,* p. 16.

20. *Ibid.,* p. 45.

21. Kothari, D.S., *Some Thoughts on Science and Religion,* New Delhi, 1977, pp. 5-6.

Chapter 14

THE LOSS OF THE GANDHIAN INITIATIVE IN INDIA

During the entire post-Gandhian era, India has not faced an over all and deep crises as it is today. The threat is less from outside and much more from its own system-collapse. Whether it is failure of army intelligence on the boarder in Kargil revealed in the enquiry report or threatening posture of criminalisation of political life or corruption in the entire social-political fields, we are in a mess. Political communalism together with casteism have become the current coin of our public life. Consumerism has almost replaced our national ethos of morality and spirituality. The worst is that we have opted for narrow sectarian nationalism in place of our traditional global vision. To conclude, it is a case of total crisis and a system-failure, for which we all are responsible.

The diagnosis has been given by the Mahatma. He said that *Seven Social Sins** will destroy us. Let us see low far they are applicable to the present conditions and find out their antidote. Let us remember that life is a unity we cannot divide it into water tight compartment called political, economic or social. Hence a person cannot do

* *Seven Social Sins* : 1. Politics without principle, 2. Wealth without work, 3. Pleasure without conscience, 4. Knowledge without character, 5. Commerce without morality, 6. Science without humanity, 7. Religion without sacrifice.

right in our department whilst attending to do wrong in another department. Life is one indivisible whole. Hence any piece-meal excercise will be futile. Besides, a total system failure needs a total revolution for which the initiative should come not from some Mahatma but from the common average men with average ability.

Politics without Principle

We have to recognise the power of politics. It controls almost everything. The Mahabharata therefore says—*Sarve dharmā Raj-dharmā ńemagrah*. Hence Gandhi, never discarded politics. Politics was not untouchable to him. Politics is like the coil of a snake. Hence in order to get out of it, we must wrath with it. But during post-Gandhian era, especially during Vinoba's Charismatic leadership, politics had almost become a taboo for the Gandhian leaders and workers. Hence, there had been ample erosion in political initiative. There was a common feeling both in the political circle as well as outside, that these Gandhian people are harmless creatures. They are not a threat to power-politics. So while the ruling party extended humanitarian help in Bhoodan movement thinking it as a Red Cross Society Work. Vinobaji had good reasons to avoid power-politics and party-politics but he also refuted the charge of being an escapist by saying that "Bhoodan is a deeper politics". Whatever might be the long term demand of politics, the immediate result was that politics was neglected and lift to the care of unscrupulous politicians. There was no principle, no true north or South, and we would not depend upon any thing. So on the one hand Bhoodan was taking a good stride, personality-cult and corruption because the hallmark of Indian politics. If Vinoba's Bhoodan would have conjoined the element of Satyagraha or non-violent resistance against injustice, things would not have deteriorated to this level. Even during Vinoba's period, we have witnessed the growth of autocracy in imposing. Emergency and deprive the hard won fundamental rights of the citizens. Vinobaji should have been vocal instead of observing silence. Thanks will go to Jaya Prakash Narain to take the budgets and fight back both corruption and despotism. On Gandhian lines. This was, I think the most powerful Gandhian initiative on national level resulting in halting the march of dictorship in India. Of course, his distant goal of ushering a total revolution on Gandhian lines met with disaster but even then we cannot ignore its contribution to usher a politics of social justice and secular democracy. J.P.'s health was too trail and precarious and he did not live long enough, hence his total revolution remained a "Paradise Lost".

Besides Vinoba's massive initiative through Bhoodan-Gandhian movement and J.P.'s most power thurst through non-violent mass-struggle, there have been some local Gandhian initiatives, about which both the intellectual elites as well as the power-oriented media have been callously neglectful. A few examples will not be out of place. In Bihar itself, seven thousands acres of land under the feudal control of the temple-priest at Bodh Gaya were taken away by J.P.'s youth army more or less on non-violent lines. So the private ownership over river water of the Ganges was liquidated through a struggle by the same youth power of J.P. in the famous *Ganga-Mukti* Movement at Kahalgaon in Bhagalpur. On the hight of the Himalayas, Sri Sunderlal Bahuguna, he internationally Known Gandhian environmentalist did usher a unique movement called *Chipko* and successfully stalled the felling of trees. Even at present he has been fighting a grim battle against the Tehridam, which falls in the sisemic zone. He is perhaps a great shinning star of Gandhian initiative. So it Baba Amte and his stormy Petral Medha Patkar raising formidable tight against unscientific Narmada dam. A valiant non-violent fighter

Sri Jaganthanji in South is fighter the combined might of the State Govt. the multinationals and the bureaucrats to save the Coastal land and its fertility by not allowing the multi-national companies to purchase fertile land to develop swarm fish. His Satyagraha-army consist of the down trodden population, mostly untouchable and women. In the Western India is Rajasthan, a young man of hardly 35 year named Rajender Singh of Tarun Bharat Sangh (Alwar) after winning the first inning against cruel exploitation and merciless marble-stone cutting has launched a massive programme of total welfare with local initiative. There are at least one hundred local Gandhian centres, where work is going on in different fields what is lacking is to coordinate their activities through a national hook.

Unfortunately, such All India Coordinating body of Gandhian constructive associations called Sarva-Seva-Sangh after passing away its great leaders like Vinoba, J.P., Dhiru Mazumdar, Dala Dharmadhikari, Anna Sahaora Buddhi, Arya Naikan etc. has become weak. This has been further adversely affected because of the vertical split during emergency. However, the credit goes to *Sarva Seva Sangh* to continue to carry the flame of Gandhian non-violent resistance against so many kinds of political, social and economic injustice. No doubt its base has shrunk and the number of its cadre has dwindled but it still preserves and carries the legacy of Gandhian initiative. The other all India Gandhian organisations like Gandhi Smarak Nidhi, Acharya Kula, Khadi Mission, Santi Seva etc. have become ineffective. But there are some Ashramas and centres like Kasturba Trust at Indore, *Brahma-Vidya-Mandir* at Paunar are example of laboratarian of Gandhian life-style and constructive programme. But they have limited scope and ambition and they hardly involve themselves in mass-action. There are some other Ashramas set up by Vinobaji and other like *Samanya Ashram* at *Bodh Gaya* under *Dwarko Bhai Sunderani*, Prathan Ashram at Pathankot under Sri Yashpal Mittal, Viswa Needan at Bangalore and Visarjan Ashram in North East, doing good work but they are not in a position to generate mass action.

The politicians and politics in India are more or less qualitatively not very different. They are all in the clutches of money, mafia and grabing power. Millions and billons of dollar of politicians are deposited in the Swiss bank and about 40% politicians have criminal records and many of them are history sheeters according to Bhuriya Committee report. Hence, what is needed is not alternative party or alternative-politics but alternative to politics. If power-game and opportunism continues, there is no escape from this morbid atmosphere. Instead of party-politics, we have to strengthen *People's Politics* by forming *Loka Samitis, Gram Sabhas* on non-party lines. To usher, organise and strengthen People's initiative is the only way out to seize the initiative and compensate loss of Gandhian initiative. As J.P. had shown the way, we have to mobilise non-violent mass political education, grass root people's organisation and mass-action programmes on real issues of the public. For this what is needed is the revival of the Gandhian spirit of 'spiritualisation of Politics' or J.P.'s "Goodness Politics" or "Politics with principle." India is on the verge of volcanic erruption of violence and anarchy because the problems of the last than has been side tracked and ignored.

The second formidable cause for the loss of Gandhian initiative is India is another wrong value of life to have "wealth without work". This refers to the practice of getting some thing for nothing, manipulating markets and assets so we donot have to work or produce added value. Today, there are professions built around making wealth without working, tax-theft, benefiting from free government programmes without carrying a far share of financial burden and enjoying all perks. Today, India is passing through a decade of greed. Politics as a profession enables one to get rich quickly.

Thanks goes to Vinoba, who has seized a very powerful economic initiative in his Bhoodan-Gramdan programme. Despite many criticisms, we have to accept the reality that more than 60 lakhs acres of land were procured through voluntary gift out of which 10-12 lakhs acres of land have been distributed among the lowest and the lost. Through much published programme of hand Reforms of the Govt. and hand Grab movement of the socialist the Communists and the Naxalites taken together have not been able to achieve even half, of this target. Any way, the Gandhians could not chick the onslaught of multinational companies in the name of globalisation and Economic Reforms. Sarva-Seva-Sangh has been trying hard to forge a forum called to fight the new economic imperialism, but so far it has not been effective. Even the raliant fighting of foreign capitalism George Fernandes etc. have only given lip service to the concept *Swadeshi* to fight out the new forms of world capitalism. The B.J.P. sponsored "Swadeshi Jagran Manch" has almost surrendered before its mentor except occasional out burst from B.J.P. labour leader Mr. Datto Pant Tengdi and veteran octogenerian Sri Nanaji Deshmukh. B.J.P. Govt. has shown unmistakable proof of its pro-capitalist stance both in matter of inside and outside the country. It has removed the ruling on urban property and has lifted any curb on import of about 3000 consumer clients. The employment position has become precarious because introduction of high-tech. Sarva Sewa Sangh has tried to oppose many such anti-people economic measures of the government but has not the appropriate organisational base. The result is that the gulf between the rich and the poor has been increasing leading to violence. Privatisation of banks, insurance, and other Public undertaking enterprises in the hand of foreign companies have dangerous political implications besides economic exploitation of the Indian masses.

7. I think that the last 15-20 years in Indian politics has been a watershed and non-issues like Mandir-Masjid, Job-reservation, etc. have dominated. The real economic issues like work for all economic equality, stress on labour intensive and low-capital industries, self-reliance have been given a good buy. Due to executive growth in consumerism, our goal of life has also been changing. So in order to usher an economic revolution, we have to organise a cultural renaissance besides creating a political will to give priority to the last Man.

Gandhi was no doubt a political giant and also a practical economist but he was essentially a high voltage cultural and moral spiritual phenomenon. Because of his moral and cultural stance, he always seized the initiative. While fighting against the British Empire, he showed utmost love and affection for them. Hence the loss of moral and spiritual initiative of the Gandhians has been the most serious problems of the Gandhian movement today. There has been loss of credibility also to a great extent is many Gandhian organisations-Khadi institution being the worst. Even at the highest levels of Sarva-Sewa-Sangh, there has been occasional complaints of forming power-cliqes and to some extent nepotism. Earlier, during Bhoodan movement, there were complaints of large-scale bogus *Dan-Patas,* or bogus-*Gramdans.* There has been power-lust in many Gandhian Stalwarts. The other faction of Sarva-Seva-Sangh, called A.I. *Rachnatmak Karya Karta Sangh* has got a pro-Congress stance while the Serva Seva Sangh is more or less anti-establishment. In short moral initiative is some what not as bright as it should better. However average moral standard is still not bad but the expectation of the people is much higher. It was the self-less and spotless integrity of Vinoba Bhave and J.P. that had given prestige and popularity to Gandhian movement. Now there is a neither close knit organisation nor a compact leadership to usher confidence. Gandhian movement need a moral initiative, an asceticism and a first practice than preach leadership. Purity of means is the first condition to usher a moral initiative. A person cannot do right in one department whilst attempting to do wrong in another department. Life is one indivisible whole. There may be barned persons in Gandhian literature but unless he has an ideal character he cannot inspire the people. An ounce of action is better than tons of words. The Gandhians have lost a powerful platform of maintaining even Basic System of education wherever it was introduced. Had if been working now, it would have provided a powerful infra-structure and man-power to take Gandhian ideas to the people. Now it has been crippled and perhaps destroyed altogether. This is perhaps the greatest loss in maintaining continuing initiative.

Concluding Remarks

Gandhism has lost its appeal in India inspite of its great historical legacy because it has lost both its creativity as well as vitality and initiative. After Gandhi's death many Gandhians paid lip services to Gandhi but it was Vinoba alone who provided both creativity and vitality to Gandhian movement. Whether the movement of Bhoodan-Gramdan was successful or not is another question. But this movement had made a mark upon our social and cultural life for quite sometime. It seemed that Gandhi was return. Bhoodan or the land-gift mission might be looked upon as largely humanitarian programme, but it is fulfilment in Gramdan had a great potentiality for a non-violent revolution. But it was a tragedy that it collapsed soon after its take off. There are multiple reasons for the failure of Gramdan-Gram Swaraj movement but major reason is that the Gandhian workers and Gandhian institutions could not cope with the demand of the movement. Neither the organisational apparatus nor the ideological base of the workers nor adequate training and appropriate resources could be mobliged. After Vinobaji, choose to be physically static at his headquarter at Paunar freeing himself from gross physical activities, heading towards a new spiritual quest called "entry into the sublime" (*Sukshmna-Pravesh*) and political diversion of most of the leaders of Bhoodan movement, towards the Bihar Movement of 1974 and consequent of vertical split in Sarvodaya movement, this grand Gandhian movement was like a God that failed. Henceforth, there has been a period of decadence in Gandhian circle and loss of initiative. Gandhism is zero minus action. So Gandhism seems to be dead and fossicized because there is lack of action. I do not think that ideologically Gandhism is weak or irrelevant but it has become without life and lustre only because of timely social action. Real Gandhism is neither pro-establishment nor anti-establishment, it is anti-social and economic injustice and pro-social change. Hence if requires vigrous action called Satyagraha. However, during post-Gandhian period, vested interest had misused Satyagraha and has reduced it to the level of *durograha*. Satyagraha minus self-purification is never safe. Hence of Gandhian movement has to pick up it strength, it has to meet both its ends—purity of character and just non-violence social action.

But there is neither Gandhi, Vinoba or J.P. who can inspire or provide leadership now. The old guards in Gandhian movement have developed natural fatigue due to long work and their old age. Hence, in order to provide initiative and action, we have to infuse new blood in the movement. J.P. had forevision and so he had given a call to the youth of India to organise on a non-partisan and non-violent basis for total revolution. He had hardly time and good health to pursue the matter and the vested interest turned 'total revolution' into a 'power game' of the worst kind. Naturally, it has got discredit. But neither its relevance not its revolutionary spirit has been lost J.P., in his long quest for social change, had tried many instrument of change. He was for long in the Kisan movement and in the Trade Union Movement also. But he found that the 'revolutionary class' of factory-labourers were more interested in their pay, pension and promotion rather than in social welfare or social revolution. Thereafter, he had a long taste of political party and even electoral politics. Being disgusted with the quagmire and selfishness of professional politicians, he joined Bhoodan-Gramdan with utmost sincerity sacrificing all their political ambivious. But here he found stagnation. So he was is search of an instrument of social change. Then towards the end of his life, he came across with the youth-power. He found that the youth have the least vestested interest and great surplus energy for being a catalyst in any programme of social revolution. They are by nature romantic and they love to risks which is necessary for any revolutionary work. The youths have also sensible hearts to listen to the sorrows and sufferings of the lowliest and the lost. They can also organise and muster in strength to fight and any injustice. The recent history was shown that the youth power has humbled many an autocrab and despots in the different parts of the world like De Gaule in France, Ayub in Pakistan or Indira Gandhi is India.

Hence it seems that if youth power can be inspired and organised properly and trained, they can remove the torpor of the entire nation. They have trust ideas and vigor, creativity and action. J.P. had organised youth-power through Indian Youth Corps and it had yielded favourable results. I think that we can provide adequate vigour and strength in the Gandhian movement by organising non-violent and non-partisan youth-power. Besides, we can also try to explore the female-power (*Stri-Shakti*), which from the better half of society. The women by nature are largely sublime, service-minded and less prone to violence and brutality. Hence, a non-violent revolution as envisaged by Gandhi will get appropriate sustenance and strength if we can organise the female power, which has been so far neglected.

Gandhism is a global phenomenon and have narrow nationalism and sectarianism in religion have no place here. If science is universal, Gandhism also must have a universal face. It is inconsistent with regimentation or fundamentalism. It is an open system. There is no place of orthodoxy or ritualism here. Gandhian movement should not make fetis of non-sense. It should try to extend its base and welcome from all walks of society to join it. Gandhi did welcome even an atheist like Professor Gora, or socialist like Lohia or J.P. and so on. Hence a touch-me-not and an over puritanistic rigid approach should be replaced by more liberal, fraternal and friendly approach. Above all, pessimism should not find a place in the minds of men. We should be trust in the ultimate triumph of truth. Due step should be enough for us. If goal is right and director of our march is correct, success is sure to come.

INDEX

H

I

J

K

L